# OWN YOUR OWN LIFE

# *Own Your Own*

# *Life*

RICHARD G. ABELL,
M.D., Ph.D.

*with*

*CORLIS WILBER ABELL*

*A Quicksilver Book*

DAVID MCKAY COMPANY, INC.

New York

*Library of Congress Cataloging in Publication Data*
Abell, Richard Gurley, 1904-
    Own your own life.
    "A Quicksilver book."
    Includes bibliographical references and index.
    1. Gestalt therapy. 2. Transactional analysis. 3. Non-
verbal communication. 4. Psychotherapy—Cases, clinical
reports, statistics. 5. Personality change. I. Abell, Corlis
Wilber, joint author. II. Title.
RC480.5.A17   616.8'914   76-4097
ISBN 0-679-50601-2

*To my patients through the years, for letting me know them, help them, and learn from them.*

# *Foreword*

In this book Dr. Richard Abell genuinely opens up both the possibility and the experience of change for all of us to see and appreciate.

Dr. Abell, who for many years has been a well-known and respected East Coast psychoanalyst, has intimately revealed here his own personal growth and change. I roared with laughter when reading about his first trip to Esalen, the human growth retreat on the Big Sur Coast of California. Dr. Abell experienced an existential shock as he arrived—replete with suit and tie, a briefcase, a hat, and stocking garters—to find a group of uninhibited, free, easygoing spirits "doing their thing." After much deliberation, he chose to stay. This experience is a classic, and I enjoy reading it aloud to my friends.

Dr. Abell moves from his own experiences to the actual setting of his consulting room, where he directly encourages his patients to grow just as he had done. He discusses the stirring case of Naomi, a Jewish woman who had lost her personal identity in Nazi-occupied Belgium. Dr. Abell had her re-experience her past traumas in order for her to gain a new, positive self-image. I personally experienced a wide variety of emotions while reading this story.

The warmth and directness of this book give me the feeling of talking with Dick and Corlis in their living room. About halfway through the book, however, I suddenly realized that this was not only the sharing of a warm, human and frequently humorous experience with the author; indeed, I was actually learning a great deal about new and potent psychological methods. Transactional Analysis, Gestalt, and nonverbal techniques are combined in synthesis with Dr. Abell's prior use of psychoanalysis. I wholeheartedly recommend this book to my clients, to my students, and to each person who wants to take charge of his or her own life.

JOHN M. DUSAY, M.D.
President,
International Transactional
Analysis Association

*San Francisco, California*
*December, 1975*

# *Acknowledgments*

*"I am a part of all I have met."*—TENNYSON: "Ulysses"

When I think of those to whom I owe a debt of thanks for helping me to write this book—beyond first of all my father and mother and brother and sister, and Uncle Arthur, my father's brother, who was a great spirit and wrote books himself—my thoughts turn to those persons, many of whom have been pioneers in their fields, who have been a source of guidance and inspiration to me. From them I learned the challenge of taking risks, the value of keeping an open mind, the importance of observing what is actually happening, and the excitement of being in the "here and now."

There was Ducky Holmes, whose real name was Jesse Herman Holmes, professor of philosophy at Swarthmore College, with whom I studied when a student there. He was the first to teach me to look for what was really there, instead of simply accepting what society said, or the culture, or newspapers, or books, or even himself. He was the first warm father figure in my life. He used to go about the environs of Philadelphia, speaking at meetings of the Society of Friends, which was always a great occasion for them. He invited me to go with him, to play the violin before he spoke.

Frank Aydelotte, president of Swarthmore when I was there, also deeply influenced me. He emphasized in his talks before the student body the importance of "intellectual curiosity." His outgoing, ebullient, enthusiastic, and erudite manner made it seem especially compelling. He took part in the Honors Conferences for the four of us who were then reading for honors in English, history, and philosophy, where there were often more professors than students, which awed me, but flattered me, too.

I want to mention Clarence McClung, formerly head of the Department of Zoology, University of Pennsylvania, with whom I studied when taking my M.A. in physiology. I remember him peering intently through his microscope, his attention centered completely on what he saw. He taught me by example the importance of total concentration. At the time, I didn't realize that this was a way of being in the "here and now." As a matter of fact, I had never heard that phrase then. But I did absorb his dedication to an unrelenting search for what was real.

I am also indebted to Eliot R. Clark, head of the Department of Anatomy at the University of Pennsylvania Medical School when I taught there. Dr. Clark was the first to discover that blood capillaries form new capillaries by sprouting. He saw this initially, under the microscope, in the tadpole's tail, and later devised a technique called a "transparent chamber," which he surgically inserted into a rabbit's ear, and in which he observed that mammalian blood capillaries also grow by sprouting: a fact important in human healing after all surgical operations and wounds. I worked with him in the development of this method for fifteen years, during the first three years of which I secured my Ph.D. in medical sciences. I taught histology, embryology, and neurology to medical students for twelve years in his department.

I was impressed with Dr. Clark's zest for observing and recording accurately. He showed me the importance of direct, immediate observation, and I came under the spell of his contagious excitement for innovation.

Another important figure to me was G.H.A. Clowes,

who, until his death a few years ago, was director of research for Eli Lilly and Company. Always interested and optimistic, he supported my work on the behavior of blood vessels in traumatic shock, a project carried out under his direction at the Marine Biological Laboratory at Woods Hole, Massachusetts, during the Second World War.

Through Dr. Clowes I met Dr. Robert Chambers, then director of the Department of Physiology at New York University. Dr. Chambers is famous for the development of his microdissection apparatus, with which he could dissect individual living cells in tissue culture and observe the effects upon them under the microscope. I lived with him and his family in informal splendor in their large house overlooking "Little Harbor" in Woods Hole when I was working there, and we got to know each other well. He was genial and, in many ways—the best ways—childlike, with his eyes open to the beauties of the macroscopic as well as the microscopic world. He, too, was a warm father figure.

I had been interested in psychology ever since having taken a course in it with Dr. Holmes at Swarthmore, but my major involvement in the field developed after I met Kenneth Appel, M.D., professor of psychiatry at the University of Pennsylvania Medical School. Dr. Appel was firmly grounded in the best of traditional knowledge and at the same time was open to new and progressive approaches. He introduced me to so many fascinating things in this field that I decided to enter medical school and become a psychiatrist.

I enrolled in medical school at the University of Pennsylvania at the age of thirty-nine, after teaching there for twelve years, and continued to teach while I worked toward my degree.

Upon completion I was awarded, with the help of Dr. Edward Strecker, then head of the Department of Psychiatry, a United States Public Health Service grant for residency training in psychiatry. I chose a residency in psychiatry at the New York State Psychiatric Institute of the Columbia Presbyterian Medical Center in New York City under Nolan D.C. Lewis, who was then director.

After my first year at Columbia, Congress decided to appropriate no more money for residency training, and I was left high and dry, only partially trained, without funds.

I contacted Dr. Joseph Wortis, then director of the Psychiatric Pavilion of Bellevue Hospital in New York City. By an unusual coincidence he knew about my successful work with a certain patient, and said I could have the one remaining opening in the Veterans' Administration Residency Training Program at Bellevue Hospital. I accepted, and this assured me of funds to complete my three years of required residency training in psychiatry. His decision to give me this residency was crucial.

During my second year of training at Bellevue, I applied for admission to the William Alanson White Psychoanalytic Institute in New York, and was accepted as a candidate for a certificate in psychoanalysis.

While there, I was deeply influenced by Clara Thompson, Frieda Fromm Reichman, Florence Powdermaker, Ralph Crowley, Leon Goldensohn (my first psychoanalyst), and Eric Fromm (who became my psychoanalyst after Dr. Goldensohn's death).

Dr. Fromm, whose original training was in classical psychoanalysis, has added many innovations to this discipline, and continues to forge ahead with new and creative ideas. He was a model for me. I never heard Dr. Fromm mention Gestalt Therapy, but as far as being in the "here and now," Dr. Fromm was the ultimate. When he looked at you, you felt taken in, lifted up, turned around, and put down right side up. I'll never forget what he said about one dream of mine. I dreamed that I was in the country and had a map showing where I was going. I lost the map but knew where I was going anyway. In my presentation of the dream I emphasized having lost the map. Dr. Fromm exclaimed, "But you know where you are going without it. How much better." I felt supported and informed by his wisdom.

Many of the faculty at Esalen Institute, Big Sur, California, played an important role in the developments that led up to writing this book. George Brown, Ph.D., Judy Brown, and Aaron Hillman gave the first workshop I attended there. Aaron taught me nonverbal techniques. George introduced me to Gestalt Therapy; he was a trainee of Fritz Perls, and his wife, Judy, had been a co-therapist with Fritz. George treated me with respect and warmth and Aaron became an important, accepting father figure for me.

I am especially appreciative of James S. Simkins, Ph.D., for his presentation of the principles of Gestalt Therapy and for his considerate, yet considered and (somewhat) frustrating treatment of me in a subsequent Esalen workshop.

I had provocative and useful experiences in the Esalen workshops I took with William Schutz, Ph.D., and Bernie Gunther. I first learned about encounter groups from Bill, and sensory awareness from Bernie.

My training in Transactional Analysis was with Robert Goulding, M.D., and Mary Edwards Goulding, M.S.W., at the Western Institute for Group and Family Therapy at Watsonville, California. This training was vital in a new plan for living that began to emerge following my experiences at Esalen. Working with the Gouldings led directly to my taking the board examinations to become a clinical member, and later a teaching member, of the International Transactional Analysis Association, and to my founding of the Transactional Analysis Institute of New York and Connecticut.

I am grateful to you, Sue Sims Bender, M.S.W., my colleague and associate, for your contagious excitement and interest in the methods and techniques of TA and Gestalt, and for your belief in the validity of what I was writing.

I am indebted to you, Owen James, for your help and friendship, and especially for playing the first part of the Bach Double Violin Concerto on the flute with me. You are a virtuoso.

Thank you, David Currier, my editor at David McKay, for your energy, persistent help and encouragement, creativity, and careful attention to significant detail.

I would also like to thank Elizabeth Shimkus for her expert typing.

Life continues to open up and expand for me, bringing new challenges and opportunities, such as the adventure of writing my first book. This brings me to Bob Silverstein of Quicksilver Books. It was Bob who suddenly said to me, "Dick, why don't you write a book about your own experiences with Transactional Analysis?" I had previously observed that Bob has an uncanny way of knowing what will succeed in the publishing world, so I just said, "All right, I will if Corlis will help me." Bob supported me in moments of frustration, when it seemed that the parts of the book would never come together. "That's all right, Dick," he would say. "There isn't any rush. Some people take seven years to write a book." That made me feel great, because at that time I had only been writing for one and a half years. Now it is two years and some, and the book is finished. Bob, you were to me a good mother and a good father and a good brother and a good sister all rolled into one. You gave me everything I could have wanted from an editor.

Now I come to Corlis, my precious and invaluable co-author. Corlis, without your gentle and loving support, your encouragement in times of despair, and your skill both as a writer and a fellow TA therapist there would have been no book.

# Introduction: Change Is a Never-ending Process

This is a book about change. About change in personality and outlook, in attitudes about ourselves and others and the world.

Do you know anyone who is satisfied with himself or herself? Who feels O.K. about his or her relations with others, who has whatever is necessary to satisfy his or her needs, who feels fulfilled, who can experience intimacy fully and without anxiety? Who is involved in activities that he or she likes, and who believes that what she or he does matters? And who is happy?

I am writing this book especially for those who want to achieve this way of being, who are not satisfied with some aspect of their lives and who want to change—to move into the existential position "I'm OK—You're OK."

This is not primarily a book about theory—at least not in the sense that I am describing methods for facilitating change which I think should work on theoretical grounds. I *know* these methods can work because they worked for me. I know they work for my patients, and they can work for you, too, if you want them to, and commit yourself to the process of change. This requires an open mind, a willingness to undergo new experiences, and a desire to learn and to change.

I am going to describe the kinds of experiences, the kinds of thinking and feeling, that can produce such change.

Although many people want to change, they don't know how to do this, partly because the reasons why they are the way they are lie outside of their awareness. In a more profound sense, they literally don't know who they are.

When people first come to see me they are usually not in touch with what they want other than to get rid of their pain. As they work with me they gradually become more aware of themselves, of who they are, and of what they really want. As this occurs, a kind of universal picture of human need and desire emerges which is rooted in the basic physiology and humanity of all of us.

What do they want? First and foremost they want to be rid of pain, confusion, and insecurity. They also want to accept themselves and their existence as important. They want to become what they are capable of becoming, and to grow and fulfill themselves. They want to be able to think freely for themselves and to be in touch with reality. They want to accept their masculinity or femininity. They want to be able to enjoy both work and play. They want to be autonomous. They want to achieve the goals they set for themselves, and be winners.

In order to achieve these things they need to undergo personality changes in which they give up unrealistic dependency upon parental and environmental support and move into the area that Fritz Perls called "self-support"; [1] that is, an acceptance of their own capability of solving their own problems.

Freud's epic-making researches leading to his formulation of the psychoanalytic method opened the way for producing such change. Building on the groundwork laid by Freud, Eric Berne and Fritz Perls, both medical doctors and originally trained as psychoanalysts, added many valuable innovations.

Eric Berne, the originator of Transactional Analysis (TA), developed, in my opinion, the best intellectual framework for understanding the human personality and how to change it, as well as a simplified vocabulary for describing it that laymen can easily grasp.

Fritz Perls, who devised Gestalt Therapy, took a different route. He became involved in finding ways of reintegrating the disowned fragments of the personality and of bringing them back into awareness. His methods center upon getting in touch with and expressing deep emotions, and experiencing the "here and now."

I have also found nonverbal communication methods useful in helping people to change. These techniques reach back beyond the origin of words into feelings that come before words, where words cannot go.

I am indebted to both Berne and Perls, but, like them, I have also gone off in my own direction. My feeling is that emotional problems are not solved exclusively either in the head or the gut, but are resolved through work which involves both, one flowing into the other. There is a very special mix which experience shows works. In this book I will show how effective this combination is in actual practice.

Dramatic and profound changes can occur, sometimes very quickly, when TA, Gestalt, and nonverbal techniques are used in one ongoing, free-flowing, therapeutic modality.

Because I myself have changed so deeply when these methods were applied to me in various groups in which I was a participant, I want to share these experiences with you. I believe that if I share with you exactly how I changed my life as a result of these new therapeutic methods, you too may feel encouraged not to accept your life as fixed and unchangeable.

There are many excellent books which deal separately with the principles of TA, Gestalt Therapy, and nonverbal communication techniques, and I advise you to read them.

Many of them are footnoted throughout this book. My purpose in writing *Own Your Own Life* is to show you how these three valuable techniques can be dynamically integrated in the therapeutic process. I am going to describe: (a) how I developed and changed; (b) how my patients changed; (c) how you can change.

If you wish to undergo personal change, there are certain specific things that you can do for yourself, and I will tell you what some of these are. The self-help exercises I describe are valid methods for increasing self-awareness. They are consciousness expanding. And for this they are valuable.

Some may wish to go further. For those who do, I believe the best way to undergo *deep personal change* is through the group methods I describe. The ideal setting for personal growth is what I would call a therapeutic environment—that is, groups of people who come together under a skilled leader specifically for the purpose of exploring old habit patterns, giving up those that are outmoded, and learning to be with each other in new and more desirable ways. They are rewarded for their new behavior with strong support—compliments, appreciations, and "strokes"—in the spontaneous responses they receive from other members of the group. In this healthy, nurturing atmosphere, members grow and develop toward self-fulfillment.

Change is a never-ending process. It is my hope that what I have written will serve as an open door through which you may pass on your own journey toward the quality of life that you want.

RICHARD G. ABELL, M.D., PH.D
*Riverside, Connecticut*
*1975*

# Contents

# CHAPTER
# 1

## *Childhood and Growing Up*

I used to be an uptight intellectual. My father was an uptight intellectual, too. Even uptighter than I was at my worst. When I was a child he used to take me out in the backyard and show me the moon through a telescope.

Hell, I didn't want to see the moon. I was lonesome. I wanted him to put his arm around me and tell me he loved me. I wanted him to say I was a fine boy, just like he'd always wanted. That I'd grow up to be a fine man, too. And live to be ninety-nine, like my grandfather—or even longer.

He didn't say any of these things. He just showed me an oval white spot on the moon and said, "That's the Sea of Tranquillity." For me it was the sea of despair. I hated it. And I hated him, too.

But I didn't let him know. That would have been too scary. I just held it in. And got uptight. And felt angry inside. Angry and awkward. Everything tight—sphincters, skin, muscles. And no fun. None.

I asked Mama why Papa never spoke about anything but the weather or some impersonal thing, and why he didn't ever eat meals with us. She just said, "Shh—let's not talk about that."

I used to wonder about a lot of things when I was little, but I learned not to ask questions. Somehow I knew our home was different from the homes of the kids I played with.

We lived in a little house in a village on the outskirts of Philadelphia—Mama and Papa, Walter, my big brother, and my little sister, Frances. Around us there were open fields to play in, and in our yard, apple trees to climb. I had a good time with the neighborhood boys, swimming in the creek nearby and playing baseball. I even had a best friend, Joe, who lived in the big house next door. He and I were pitcher and catcher on the baseball team, leaders of the gang, and proud of it. But all of the pleasure and excitement of having friends ended as soon as I got home. I got the unspoken message that home was not a place to have a good time; and that the important things in life were to work hard and study and be a success. From the family atmosphere, and from the way Papa treated me—and Mama went along with it—I learned that to be close or have fun or be spontaneous was not safe.

Papa was, in fact, a recluse. Except for his business, he had cut himself off from the outside world. No visitors came to the house, because Papa forbade it, and his word was law to us. Mother was naturally outgoing and sociable, but no neighbor ever dropped in for a cup of coffee. She spent most of her time in the kitchen, like a short-order cook, as the family never sat down to a meal together. We all lived on separate schedules, taking our cues on how to live from Papa. He would come home from work, eat in solitary silence, and retire to his room to read and study. Sometimes he would repair secondhand violins that he bought in pawn shops for five or six dollars. He loved his old violins.

I wanted him to love me.

Now, as I look back on the unhappy years of my childhood, I can understand why Papa was unable to give me the love and attention I needed. I know now what I had no way of knowing then—that he was an unusually brilliant and talented man who was disappointed in his own life. When he was thirteen years old, he was put out to work on a farm. His only companion was a deaf-and-dumb hired hand. My God, I don't know how he survived. But he did, and he turned over most of his meager earnings to his father to help support his eleven brothers and sisters.

In spite of the demands on him, he managed to work his way through Yale. He was a natural scholar, and it isn't surprising that he was offered an instructorship, leading toward a doctorate in astronomy at Yale. But he felt obliged to turn it down because of the continued need for money at home. He decided to get a master's degree in engineering instead of following his natural inclination. This decision was fateful, since he settled for a profession that he didn't really like; and for the rest of his life, as an employee of a large electrical company, he failed to make much money anyway.

In addition to helping his family, he sent his younger brother, Arthur, to Germany to study with the renowned violinist, Joseph Joachim. Arthur became an internationally known music critic, surrounded by celebrities. My father, who, as I told you, loved the violin, taught himself to play "Old Black Joe." But he saw to it that I had violin lessons, and I, too, love the violin. It has been a continuing source of joy in my life.

But when I was a little boy, I did not realize that the music lessons were his gift of love to me. It was the best he could do—he couldn't show tender feelings to anyone. In fact, he became so bitter and resentful over the continued demands of his family that he finally broke off all connection with them. The break was so complete that I never knew, until I was in college, that papa had any relatives. It was then that Mama broke the tight censorship and told me what had happened.

Now, I understand his disappointment and frustration; but all I knew as a child was what it was like to live in a family centered about a disillusioned man turned in on himself. I didn't know that the way Papa treated me would have such far-reaching effects. I didn't know that his going about his own life and ignoring me was what Eric Berne, the founder of Transactional Analysis, would call a " 'Don't exist' injunction." I wasn't aware that I made an early decision, "I'll show you if it kills me," meaning—in my case— 'I'll work hard and study and do so well that you'll have to notice me, Papa, even if I die in the attempt."

By the time I entered high school, the spontaneous, fun-loving kid in me, which in Transactional Analysis language is called the Free Child, was almost completely squelched. I wanted so much to be close, to be accepted by my classmates, but I didn't know how.

In our house, there had never been the fun of sharing daily news and experiences over the family dinner table, or the excitement of parties or company; no feeling of celebration over holidays and birthdays; no hugging and touching, or displays of affection; no kidding or joking or foolishness. Life was serious, and the house was quiet, as we went our separate ways. As you can see, I wasn't very well equipped to enter the adolescent fray. My best friend, Joe, began dating girls, and we drifted apart. I felt anxious and awkward and shy. I didn't know how to participate in the sociable banter that flowed around me. Somehow I was outside the magic circle. I wanted to be friends with my classmates, but I felt that I was boring. Silently I yearned for the most beautiful girl in the class—at a safe distance.

Well, I went through high school, college, graduate school, and medical school, not being really close to anyone, not showing my feelings, and feeling lonely and isolated. One thing I knew how to do well was to study hard and get good grades. I was always at the top of my class, and received scholarships and scholastic honors. Now, surely, Papa would be pleased and notice me. He never did. I wasn't happy. He didn't notice that either.

Of course, the reason I wasn't able to be close to people is clear to me now. I was taught by my father, and by my early family life, how not to be close and how not to express my feelings. Even during my psychoanalytic training, these messages weren't entirely reversed. It isn't strange, there-fore, that as recently as seven years ago I still wasn't completely comfortable with myself and my colleagues, even though I was a successful psychoanalyst.

From the outside, the picture looked good. Here I was, with a lucrative practice, doing the work I liked, married to a warm and affectionate woman, and living in Connecticut in our recently purchased home, "Landfall," which we loved. I commuted to my office in New York and over the weekend saw a few patients at home. I must have been doing *some* things right. I was. I was making a living. I was always successful with patients. That had been the case even with the first patients I had treated during my residency training at the New York State Psychiatric Institute at the Columbia Presbyterian Medical Center. The feeling for how to help patients seemed almost to be inborn with me, perhaps because in a certain sense I *had been* where they *were* and so respected their position. They were OK with me. I respected their identity, whatever it was. I loved them, in a sense, just for being. An unconditional, masterful stroke, to use Transactional Analysis language, and very helpful to them. Most of them had never had that.

Yet in spite of this worldly success—the result of working hard, as my father had taught me to do—in spite of my success with patients, I somehow didn't feel that I belonged with my colleagues socially.

What I really felt with them was "I'm not OK—You're OK." I tried to disguise this from them by telling them how busy I was, or about the last paper I had written, or by asking them for information which I carefully put down in a little notebook I always carried.

As I learned later from Transactional Analysis theory, this was the Adapted Child in me, still wanting to be noticed and approved, as I had wanted to be noticed by Papa. It didn't work then, because he was unable to notice me, and it didn't work now, with my colleagues. I didn't know why.

Now, seven years later, I do know why. And I am a

changed man. I am relaxed and happy, and the horizons of my life continue to expand. I live in a house on a hill, surrounded by pine trees, overlooking Long Island Sound. With a four-mile view from the deck over the countryside in one direction and a view of the Sound in another; with sunshine on my face, blue sky and white clouds above, and one of my favorite sounds in my ears—the screech of the wheeling seagulls. One of my favorite sounds—yes. Perhaps even more favorite—the soft, reassuring, gay, and seductive laugh that I hear through the living room door as I write. That is my co-author's laugh. For some reason she doesn't want to be introduced simply as my wife, even though she is. She has her own identity first, she says. And she's right. But to introduce her as my co-author—that's a little different. I'll see if that's OK with her.

It is. And I'm OK with her, too. And with my patients and trainees and colleagues. And most important—with myself.

I no longer feel awkward at parties, anxious about what to say. I love parties. For I have become my own man, and what I say is interesting because it comes out of my own identity. If anyone thinks it isn't—that's his responsibility!

Perhaps the thing that I cherish most of all—in what I call my new life—is intimacy. I have learned how to be intimate. To be close to a few people I really care about. To share personal feelings, to trust, to love without reservation.

Now life is exciting, fulfilling.

Somewhere between my earlier desolation and my present happiness lies the answer to owning my own life.

I am going to tell you step by step what happened, for I know—and you will be surprised. Because changing injunctions that teach "Don't exist" and "Don't be close" and "Don't show your feelings" into "Life is fulfilling and exciting," "Closeness is precious and rewarding," and "To show your feelings is a freeing experience" is quite a trick. But it can be done. And the reason I'm writing this book is to tell you that if you want to own your own life, you can do it too.

Let's go back now, to seven years ago, when I wanted to change, but didn't know how.

"Somewhere, somehow, there must be some way of breaking out of this impasse," I thought. Then I heard about Fritz Perls' work in Gestalt Therapy at Esalen Institute. I read his Gestalt prayer: [1]

I do my thing, and you do your thing.
I am not in this world to live up to your expectations
And you are not in this world to live up to mine.
You are you and I am I,
And if by chance we find each other, it's beautiful.
If not, it can't be helped.*

The idea that I am not in this world to live up to anyone's expectations relieved me and gave me a vague sense of peace. Perhaps, I thought, Gestalt Therapy will offer me some way out of my position of wanting to change but not knowing how. Fritz Perls' words, "Lose your head and come to your senses," kept running through my mind.

I've never done that, I thought. I'm going to try it.

With hope and misgiving, at the age of sixty-six, I signed up for two workshops at Esalen Institute in Big Sur, California, in the summer of 1969.

With this signature I began a quest to find the "I" in me, which turned up many risky vicissitudes and some unexpected pleasures.

# CHAPTER
# 2

## Esalen

I climbed out of the taxi that brought me the fifty miles from the Monterey airport to Big Sur—a drive along one of the most spectacular coastlines in the world—and looked around, feeling anxious and out of place.

As those of you who have been to Esalen know, it is located on a narrow plateau overlooking the Pacific Ocean. Backdropped by a series of high, brown, rolling hills, its green lawns extend to a series of cliffs which plunge abruptly into the sea. I rested my eyes for a moment on the ocean, sparkling in the late afternoon sun, and on the breath-taking expanse of the horizon which seemed to stretch to infinity.

Somewhat reassured, I looked at the main lodge, which was directly in front of me, and studied the small, rustic cabins, scattered in rows up the hillside, linked by casual paths. Each, I noticed, had its own particular view of the ocean.

So this is Esalen, I thought. I began to feel a little hot in the July sun. I was wearing a gray flannel suit, stocking garters, black shoes, a white shirt, and, of course, a tie. In one hand I clutched a briefcase, heavy with books and papers. In the other I held a furled umbrella, against the possibility of rain. (I learned later that it never rains in July in Big Sur.)

I had arrived without luggage, which you may interpret symbolically if you like. At any rate, my bags had been delayed, mislaid, lost or stolen somewhere between New York and Monterey. I had nothing to wear except what was on my back, and my New York Fifth Avenue tailoring made me feel uncomfortably conspicuous. Lounging on the porch rail next to the office door were several bearded young men. Their hair was long, their shirts were open to the waist, their feet were in sandals. One or two wore beads. The men were talking quietly to some pretty girls. I noticed their lovely long hair, and their long dresses, which touched their bare ankles. I noticed particularly the look of quiet peace upon their faces.

I put down my briefcase and umbrella and walked to the other end of the lodge. There, on a large, open deck a man knelt on one knee, with his arms outstretched to the sky. Just beyond him a man and woman stood in a relaxed embrace, looking intently into each other's eyes.

My God, I thought, they are certainly strange-looking people. What am I doing here?

Later I learned from Aaron Hillman, one of the instructors in my first course, that he had been watching my arrival and was asking himself, My God, what have we here?

Should I go or stay? I communed with myself. One thing is true of me. If I start a project, if I commit myself, I stay with it until it is finished. Perhaps this is a message handed down in our family from my forebears, who were sea captains out of Salem: "Stick with the ship, and bring it through the storm." There might be rough sailing ahead, in strange and perhaps dangerous waters, but I would stick with the ship. I would stay. I turned, went into the office and registered. I was assigned to the cabin where I was to live the next two weeks, during which I would undergo some of the most bewildering and beautiful experiences of my life.

Before I attended my first workshop that evening, I took the Esalen catalogue out of my briefcase and checked again, by the dim light in the cabin, the course I was about to embark upon. (I was a day late, because of the pressure of several appointments and meetings which could not be postponed.) The description sounded reassuringly reasonable and adult. No nude marathons, no dancing in the moonlight with vine leaves in the hair; "Training workshop for affective learning and humanistic education," said the catalogue. "Descriptions, theory and practice in the affective domain: (a) nonverbal communication, (b) dyadic interpersonal relationship, (c) group process, (d) group leadership, (e) sensory awakening, (f) existential and humanistic psychology based on the Gestalt Therapy of Fritz Perls ... the integration of affective learning with cognitive or intellectual dimensions of learning. ..." The workshop was conducted under the leadership of George and Judy Brown, Aaron Hillman, and Gloria Siemons, and was offered primarily to teachers, church-affiliated leaders, social workers and others professionally concerned with human relationships. Splendid, I thought. Why should I be nervous?

I must remind you now that I have shared with you my innermost feelings about myself. If any of my professional colleagues had asked me why I was going to Esalen, I would have said that I was interested in learning new techniques, such as nonverbal communication, sensory awareness, encounter, and Gestalt Therapy, as methods which, in conjunction with psychoanalytic therapy, might prove useful in facilitating change in my patients. And this statement would have been true. I am an experimenter and an innovator, and I am willing to take risks. Any theory or method that will expand or sharpen my professional skills is of primary importance to me. I was not as fully aware then, as I am now, of the depth of my longing to change, and the hope that somehow I might find the answer at Esalen.

It was time for the session to begin. I picked my way

down the dark path to a big cabin with glass doors that opened to the sea and the night breeze. About forty people lounged in a circle on cushions, or leaned against the wall, or against each other. I sat down beside an attractive brunette and introduced myself. Her name was Peggy, and she was an English teacher from Denver, she told me.

The leader of the group tonight was Aaron Hillman. I liked his wise, merry eyes and his handsome, white beard. With no didactic explanations whatsoever, he started the group on a nonverbal communication exercise.

I am going to give you his instructions just as he gave them to the group; you may want to try them sometime and see what happens.

"Pick a partner," Aaron said, "preferably of the opposite sex. Hold one hand, palm out, against the palm of your partner's hand, and get to know your partner's hand with your eyes closed, and without talking. Say hello, have a conversation, have a quarrel, make up, say good-bye. Then open your eyes and share your feelings with your partner."

... Have a hand-to-hand conversation with a perfect stranger? This was a clear-cut directive to be close, to do exactly the opposite of my father's injunction, "Don't be close." Well, I was here to learn new techniques, wasn't I?

I turned to Peggy and she gently put her palm against mine. After finishing the exercise I said to her, "Your hand is very soft, warm, affectionate, creative in the manner of your exploration, strong at times, at other times gentle. I liked the exercise very much."

She shared with me her own feelings about my hand. "Your hand is strong. You took charge. I liked that. Your skin is soft, too. Your movements are smooth and unhurried. Your hand was relaxed, gentle, and affectionate."

I hadn't known that about my hand. This was the beginning of a series of intense experiences which helped me to get rid of feelings implanted in me by my father that it is dangerous to be close.

I was deeply impressed. I cannot, as a matter of fact,

overstate the importance of this simple, nonverbal exercise and our mutual sharing of feelings. It began the change in me toward a new kind of existence.

"Pick another partner and do it again," Aaron said.

I did, with growing confidence.

"Now pick another partner, and get to know your partner without talking, and with your eyes closed. Feel your partner's hair, feel the texture of her hair, feel her scalp, feel her hairline, feel your partner's forehead, feel her eyebrows, feel her eyelashes, feel her nose, feel her lips, feel her cheeks, feel her ears and all the little curves and crevices, feel her chin, feel under her chin, feel her neck (gently, don't choke her), feel her shoulders and the curve of the shoulders. Feel how the shoulders connect with the neck and with the body—all the curves. Feel her chest. Notice her breathing, notice the rhythm of her breathing. Feel the solidity of the hips. Feel your partner's legs and feet. Feel each toe. Examine the instep of the arch. Then open your eyes and share your feelings with your partner."

I did everything as directed and contradicted every injunction that I got from my father—with permission. I didn't realize it then, but I see it now: the importance of the permission. It's all right to touch, it's all right to be close, it's all right to share feelings. Not only is it all right—*do it:* that's the message. From an authority that I considered more knowledgeable than my father.

I was thrilled and excited with the experience, and my partner, Anne, enjoyed it, too. She said, "Your hands are gentle and warm. I liked the experience."

We did one more exercise that evening. "Pick another partner," Aaron said. "Then look directly into her or his eyes for about one minute. Then share your feelings."

I did. It was another new experience in closeness. Pleasant for both of us.

I was feeling high by the end of the evening.

Before I went to Esalen I had heard about the famous hot sulfur baths, where the participants in the workshops—

seminarians—went bathing in the nude. I decided ahead of time that this was not for me. No sir! Bathing in the nude with strange women? Unthinkable. Anyway, I would probably get an erection and be terribly embarrassed.

To make doubly sure that I wouldn't take a chance on the nude baths, I had a mole taken off my chest just before I left New York for Esalen. I knew the cauterized area wouldn't be healed when I got there. And it wasn't.

As we left the workshop room Peggy came up to me and said, "Are you going down to the baths?"

I gulped. I looked at her questioningly. She looked friendly, matter-of-fact.

"I hadn't planned to," I said. I looked at her again.

"Everybody does," she said. "One-half of the bath house is reserved for our class."

She left.

I was in a turmoil. The feeling began to develop. No doubt about it—I wanted to go. But what about that unhealed wound? Then I thought, "The sulfur will be good for it." Bless the power of rationalization. I smeared some Vaseline over the unhealed area and left for the baths. As it turned out, no wound ever healed quicker!

I remember the walk to the baths as if it were right now. The path ran down the side of a cliff overlooking the Pacific Ocean. There was a new moon, its pale light reflected in the water. A couple of hundred feet below I could see the waves foaming through craggy rocks and breaking on the narrow, stony beach. The delightful, recurrent roar of the breakers was faint, but distinct. The air was cool, almost chilly, even though it was the last week in July. Overhead, the stars were bright.

I picked my way along that uneven, rocky path carefully, using my flashlight. One misstep could have meant curtains. Nobody, I thought, protects you from anything around here.

The fact is, I liked that funny little rough path and its closeness to nature. And I liked not being protected.

In the blackness, I first became aware that I was finally approaching the baths by the smell of sulfur. Not a pleasant smell, exactly. But not unpleasant, either. Distinct, but not too strong.

A low building had been built around the baths, of which, I discovered, there were four, each about eight feet square and made of concrete.

The first decision I had to make after I entered the narrow passageway leading to the baths was whether to go to the right or the left when I came to a blind end. I felt a little like a rat in a maze, entering Hades. It was dark, damp, and the smell of sulfur was everywhere.

I went to the left, down some concrete stairs, and suddenly came to a large room about thirty-five feet long and twenty-five feet wide, completely open on one side to the ocean, the new moon, and the stars. There was very little light in the room. I had to use my flashlight (keeping it discreetly focused on the floor) to find a dry place to leave my clothes—a massage table, as I found out later.

I stood by the table, in the dark, undressing; and what was going through my head? Was it the fear of getting an erection? Not at all. It was how to keep my clothes from getting wet with the sulfur water that was running everywhere over the concrete floor, and—why was it taking me so long to get undressed?

I tossed my underpants on the table, at last, and with them, a certain psychological reticence. By this time my eyes had become somewhat accustomed to the dark, and I could see a faint outline of a bath with some figures in it, but I couldn't tell who.

"Hello," I called.

"Hello," Peggy called back. I walked in the direction of her voice, stepped over the side of the bath, and settled into the hot water. I looked around.

At the far corner of the bath, next to the wall, was a candle, flickering. Faintly outlined against it were the head and shoulders of a girl. I could see the soft roundness of the top of her breasts above the water, and the free flow of her hair as it fell gracefully over her shoulders.

I looked around some more. Next to me was a man.

"I'm Dick Abell," I said.

"I'm John Forman," he replied. "Where are you from?"

"New York."

"That's a long way off," he said.

I thought, Here I am in the nude, sitting in a bath, having a conversation exactly as I would if I were fully dressed.

Across the pool I heard two voices, one a man's voice, the other a woman's, talking about the beauties of the Big Sur coastline, along which they had both driven on their way to Esalen. Next to John was Peggy. I paddled over to her (the water was about three feet deep) and we sat next to each other, with our backs against the wall of the bath.

"Hello," I said again.

"Hi," she said. "I'm glad you decided to come down. How are you feeling about it?"

"Great," I said.

I was sitting in a bath, nude, beside a girl who was also nude, carrying on a conversation with her, just as if we were dressed. I began to think that if one has respect for where another person is, for her identity, it doesn't make much difference whether one is dressed or not. My fear of nudity began to go away.

The next morning our section gathered in the main conference room. Since my suitcase had still not arrived from the airport, I was obliged to appear in my gray flannel suit, and I felt uncomfortable in the casual, relaxed atmosphere of the group. What can I do? I thought. I rolled my slacks up to my knees and took off my shoes and socks. Immediately I felt better. Aaron began the workshop with a body-awareness experience.

"Sit straight up in your chair," he said, "and plant your feet firmly on the floor. Feel the pressure of your feet against the floor and the pressure of the floor against your feet. Be aware of each toe, one at a time. Be aware of your ankles and how they feel. Be aware of the muscles of your legs, back, and front. Center on your knee joints. Be aware of the kinesthetic sensations in your knee joints, of the feelings in your thighs, of the sensations in your hips, each one of your backbones, as you go from the bottom of your spine to the top of it. Be aware of the muscles of your back. Concentrate on where your skull fastens onto your spine. Turn your head back and forth, and feel the sensations at the back of your skull. Feel the skin on your face, your lips, your cheeks, your nose, your forehead, your ears. Pay attention to the sensations in your scalp. Notice your breathing. Be aware of its rhythms. Breathe in deeply and feel the air rush into your lungs. Feel the sensations in your shoulders, in your upper arm, in your elbow joint, in your lower arm, in your wrist, in your hand, in each finger."

This was my first body-awareness exercise, and my first experience of an exercise designed to focus my mind on the "here and now," a phrase that was to become more and more meaningful to me as time went on.

After the exercise I felt strangely refreshed; I didn't know why. Now I know that when the mind is focused on the "here and now," anxiety drops away.

Aaron started the next exercise by saying, "I'm Moses, who are you? Be anyone you want to be, from any time in history."

We went around the circle from left to right. "I'm Dorothy, in *The Wizard of Oz*," said one girl. "I'm Abraham Maslow," I said, feeling very important and expansive. Good old Abe, modest Abe, brilliant Abe, creative Abe, formerly head of the Department of Psychology at Brandeis University, one of the founders of the Human Potential Movement and a key figure in the establishment of Esalen. His book *Motivation and Personality* was on the list of reading I assigned when I was teaching mental hygiene to the freshman class at Barnard College. The girls loved what he wrote. I loved him for himself.

It was largely through his influence that I was able to experience a "rebirth" at Esalen. He is now dead, but as I write this, I look out of my Connecticut study window into the expansive sky, with the sun rising behind the pine trees, and three birds flying in formation, and I feel his presence.

I first met Abe at a meeting of the Academy of Psychoanalysis, where he was a keynote speaker. I was excited by his pioneering work on "the self-actualizing person," and he became interested in me through my involvement in mass media.

"How can we reach and influence more people—millions?" he asked me.

"Through television" I told him. "I had a television program on ABC-TV on their full network in 1960-61. It was a half-hour show, five days a week. It was a group therapy program—the first group therapy show on the air. Over four million people looked at it every day."

After that we became friends. He used to invite me up to Brandeis University, in the early sixties, to show a video tape of one of my group therapy sessions to his psychology class of fourth-year students. Just before he died I received a beautiful letter from him. There was a liberated man—open, friendly, direct. I admired Abe—wanted to be more like him.

Some of these thoughts and feelings went through my head as I said to Aaron, "I am Abraham Maslow." I felt a warm, expansive glow. Aaron had given me "permission" to be something I had wanted to be for a long time. In fantasy, yes. But fantasy, after all, often precedes reality.

At lunch that day in the dining room at Esalen, by a big window overlooking the Pacific Ocean, I met Adeline. She was to play a crucial part in my "humanization." A brunette. Beautiful dark-brown hair, cut just above her shoulders. Sparkling brown eyes. A smile that lit the room.

I sat next to her, and as we ate we began to talk. "What did you do the first day?" I asked. "I'm sorry I had to miss it."

"We went on a blind walk," Adeline said, smiling at me.

"What in the world is a blind walk?"

"You pick a partner, close your eyes, and hold out your hand. Your partner leads you around to sensory experiences. While you're exploring something—like a rose petal, or somebody's head—your partner lets go of your hand. When you've finished, you hold out your hand and she takes you on to more experiences."

"Oh," I said. "I'm sorry I missed that."

"I'll take you on a blind walk," Adeline said. We finished lunch.

"How about now?" I said.

It was a good time. Seminarians were sitting on the lawn, talking in couples and in groups, or leisurely walking about, looking at the ocean and watching the long Pacific swells come rolling gracefully in to finally break precipitously on the narrow stony beach two hundred feet below. Several people were lying at the edge of the free-formed swimming pool, and a few were swimming.

We went onto the lawn at the foot of the stone steps from the deck of the main building. I closed my eyes and put out my hand. Adeline took it. She put my hand first on something cold and hard. I avoided stereotyping it. I wanted to experience it. Cold, hard, slightly rough, obliquely placed in space—it was the iron rail of the stairs leading from the deck to the lawn. But that was the least important thing about it for me, for this exercise. What I was trying to do was experience the object as if I were coming across it for the first time. To *feel* the experience. Once a thing is conceptualized, the tendency is to say, "That is an iron rail," toss it into the basket with all the other stereotypes, and forget about it. That's the reverse of what this exercise is for.

After finishing my examination, I held out my hand, eyes still closed. *Adeline took my hand.* That was the crucial thing. *Adeline took my hand; she was there.* As my father had never been there. She affirmed my existence. I felt that her taking my hand was a "Do exist" message. And it happened repeatedly that afternoon.

Next Adeline placed my hand on the grass. I felt its coolness, the matted, springy body of it. The grass at Esalen is not ordinary grass. It is like a four-inch-deep resilient mattress. I felt the individual intertwined strands. I felt the cool earth.

I held out my hand. Adeline placed it on something smooth and silky. I ran my fingers through it and it felt good. It was the hair of a girl. I explored her face, as in the workshop exercise.

I held out my hand; *Adeline took it.* The next thing I knew my hand was immersed in a slightly cool, soft liquid. I swished my hand through it, and ran it between my fingers. It felt caressing and enveloping. It was the water of the swimming pool.

Suddenly I heard a noise like a seal bellowing and felt something soft and warm under my hand. I was taken completely by surprise, and was for a moment nonplussed. It was almost round, and the soft mat on top of it was made up of thousands of fine strands. It was the head of Don, a colleague in the workshop who was pretending to be a seal.

I put out my hand again. *Adeline took it.* It was two o'clock and time to start the afternoon session, so we terminated.

In this walk it became very clear that, for me, inanimate objects were much less interesting to touch than living ones; that touching another person brings a satisfaction not to be found in any other way; that the injunctions "Don't be close," "Don't touch" that I got from my father were purely personal with him and that I didn't need to control my behavior by his directions any longer. And especially, Adeline's *always* taking my hand when I held it out had a profound meaning for me.

By this time in the workshop I had come to know most of the people, and was becoming fond of them—more so than any other group I had ever known, either in high school or in college. And I could tell from the way most of them responded to me that I was well liked. This was beginning to reach me and was having a deep effect on me. My up-tightness was loosening.

My next experience was one of the most crucial of the entire workshop. The whole class gathered on the lawn in the sunshine. The exercise was conducted by Gloria, one of the other leaders. "Each of you take a sheet," Gloria said. "You are to be born under the sheet; feel what it's like just to be born; begin to move around and explore the environment and gradually grow up. I'll give the directions. Get under your sheet now."

I got under my sheet. "Now imagine that you are being born." I curled up in the fetal position and made little whimpering noises and felt completely helpless. It was a good feeling, feeling helpless and not feeling afraid.

"Now begin to move around with your sheet over you, just a little at a time, and explore the environment." I began to move my body, my hands, my feet, still lying down. Then I began slowly crawling around. I couldn't see anything around me because of the sheet, so I began to investigate the grass. It was quite dark under that sheet. I tried to take the point of view of a baby toward the end of the first year, for whom the world is new, unexplored.

"Now move more, until you bump into something or someone. Then explore that," Gloria said. The purpose of the sheet was to block stereotyping by sight. I bumped into a big irregular object, very muscular and solid. A man. I moved on. I bumped into a not so big and not so solid object. A woman. I stayed awhile, still under my separate sheet. I kept on bumping for about fifteen minutes until I was beginning to feel pretty grown up. Just before the exercise ended, I had the impulse to grab the last girl I bumped into and roll over and over again in the deep grass, down the slight hill that we were on. I did, and we laughed. I was still under my sheet and couldn't see her. By the time I was disentangled she was gone.

That night when the whole group of forty were as-sembled, before George Brown started the meeting, I asked George if I could make an announcement.

"This afternoon," I said, "after being born under a sheet and growing up, I grabbed a girl and rolled over and over with her down the hill. It was a great experience for me. One of the best. But I don't know who she was. If she knows who I am, would she please introduce herself to me?"

Everyone laughed. A very pretty girl spoke up. "I'm the one," she said. "I'm Jean."

"Thank you," I said, "for the great experience." I thought I did pretty well. A strange thought for me, but becoming more familiar.

I want to go back now to the lawn, on that beautiful afternoon in July 1969, just after we finished the experience of being born.

Esalen is the only place in the world that I know of where kids come and watch the adults in unstructured play. We had an admiring group of four-year-olds. After we finished and the sheets were being collected and put in a pile, they came over to us and asked if we would bounce them up in the air on the sheets. We did and we were all having a fine time, laughing and yelling, when one of the parents came running over and said, "Don't do that. The sheets might tear and our children might get hurt." He was in his Parent ego state, all right, and I could see the beginning of "The world's a dangerous place, be careful," for his children, but we complied.

After the kids left with their parents, I lay down on one of the sheets and said to Jim, a blond, curly haired giant and one of the men I felt closest to in the group, "Jim, now toss me up and down."

"OK," Jim said, not to be outdone, "we will." He and about sixteen of the others stood together for a moment talking in low voices. I lay there in anticipation, wondering what was going to happen. I was fully dressed, except that I had taken off my wristwatch, glasses and shoes.

Jim came over with the others. "Pick him up," Jim said. I lay still, resolved to let happen what would happen. The group lined up, eight people on each side of me, picked me up, and held me at arm's length over their heads. They all began to chant some chant, the words of which I couldn't understand—if there were any words. Then they began to move slowly. I wasn't thinking about where they were going. I was feeling great. I was chanting, too, by that time. Gradually it dawned on me that they were walking toward the pool. "No," I yelled. "Not that!" only half playfully.

"Yes, yes, yes," they all chanted in unison. I was helpless. We were at the edge of the pool. I looked down, from what seemed to be about twenty-five feet. I saw the concrete edge of the pool directly under me. I thought, "If they don't throw me all the way out, and I fall on that edge, I'll break my back. Shall I yell to Jim to stop, to let me down?"

It happened then, in that instant, that I made one of the most crucial decisions of my life. "I'm going to let it happen. I'm just going to see what happens." My God, if my father had seen me he would have had a heart attack.

"One," Jim yelled. The group swayed me back.

"Two," Jim said. The group got ready.

"Three!" Jim yelled.

A tremendous shove . . . I was high in the air, clothes and all, well beyond the edge of the pool. Below me the little bright ripples of the pool glistened in the sun.

SPLASH! I was in.

I came up from under the water, yelling. I felt great. Everybody was yelling and laughing. I jumped over the side of the pool and threw every one of those sixteen people, including Jim, into the pool, clothes and all. I didn't meet much resistance; they were ready. We were all having fun.

After it was over, I took off my clothes, down to my shorts, and hung them up to dry on the iron rail I had felt earlier in the day. I was walking to my room clad only in my shorts, to get some dry clothes, when I met Aaron. "My God, Dick," he said, "every time I see you, you have fewer clothes on."

At supper I sat next to Adeline. She was in the other section of the class and didn't know what had happened to me that afternoon. "I was thrown in the pool," I said excitedly. "It was great." The sun was setting over the ocean as we ate. "Let's go out on the edge of the cliff and watch it set," I said. We walked across the lawn, hand in hand, picked a comfortable spot, and sat quietly together. Far below the waves came foaming in, breaking on the narrow, pebbly beach. As they receded, the rounded pebbles rolled over each other, making a faint clicking sound in the stillness.

California sunsets are not like sunsets on the East Coast, where the sky is crimson and the sun sinks flaming into night. California sunsets in the Big Sur area are more subdued—a pale, golden yellow. We watched intently while the waves foamed and the pebbles clicked, and the sun sank quietly into the Pacific.

"Adeline," I said, "I would like to get to know you better. I don't want to go to bed with you. It isn't sex I want. I want to learn to be close." She looked at me in the dusk, carefully, as if she wanted to see if what I said was true. "I have trouble being close, too," she said. "And when someone tries to get close to me I pull away. Don't let me." We went back to the dining room and finished our supper.

The next morning our group assembled again at ten o'clock. Aaron said, "Form a line. Put your arms on the shoulders of the person in front of you. I'll lead." Aaron led us around the room. We were like a long, writhing boa constrictor. "Make a noise like an animal," Aaron directed. We each began to growl or shriek or bleat or meow, according to the animal of our choice.

Aaron continued with his directions. "Form one group with the first half of the line," he said. "And another with the second, at opposite ends of the room. This group has "it" he said, and the other group has to get "it." I was in the group that had to go and get "it." The members of my group all looked at the other group, sizing them up. They had formed a tightly interwoven close-knit circle, to protect "it." We all went over in a bunch to try to break in and get "it." But the other side was very determined, and we had a hard time. Finally, I flung myself over the top of the circle and toppled inside. I began grabbing "it" and stuffing it in my pockets; and the others were grabbing me. Then my team suddenly departed after getting their share of "it" and left me in the center of the other group, a captive. I fought, I struggled and I finally broke out.

It may seem to you that the kind of things I have been describing are kid stuff, inconsequential, not worthy of adults; that instead we should have been discussing serious psychological problems in earnest little groups. Nothing could be further from the truth, so far as I am concerned. I wanted to get *away* from intellectual discussions, which are already two steps removed from raw feelings—first by the use of symbols (words) and second by conceptualization, abstraction. I wanted to experience *feeling*. I couldn't do it by talking about feelings, only by experiencing them. How could I best experience feelings? By participating in exercises which are designed to elicit feelings. And they did.

The Esalen setup is a controlled environment for the facilitation of personal growth, and it was working very well for me. I was getting beneath intellectualization to feeling. I could yell, I could laugh; I was beginning to feel comfortable with people. I could touch others, I could share my feelings. I was starting to overcome the effect of my father's "Don't be close" and "Don't show your feelings" injunctions. Even the pain from the "Don't exist" injunction was beginning to go away. I was very pleased.

It was now Saturday at lunch. The first six-day workshop that I had come to Esalen to take was over. The air was filled with a mixture of excitement and, already, slight feelings of nostalgia and regret at leaving. There were too many members in our group for all of us to sit at one table, but those of us who had become especially close managed to be together for this last lunch.

I sat next to Adeline. "Adeline," I said, taking her hand in mine, "you will probably never know how much being with

you has meant to me. I hope we'll see each other again."
She squeezed my hand affectionately.

We *have* seen each other again several times—at various
workshops at Esalen and at the National Training Laboratory in Bethel, Maine. Last summer Adeline and her new
husband visited Corlis and me in Connecticut.

Jim, the curly haired giant who engineered my being
thrown into the pool, was sitting on my left. "Jim," I said,
putting my hand on his shoulder, "I'll never forget being
suspended in the air above the pool for about one-tenth of a
second, like a bird. It was a great experience." We talked
casually and jokingly.

After lunch I held Adeline close to me for a few short,
sweet seconds, and then I hugged Jim, and then the three of
us hugged each other. After that we separated.

The second workshop I had signed up for began Sunday
night at nine o'clock in Fritz Perls' former cabin—the one he
lived in while working at Esalen, before he went to Canada
and founded his own institute. This workshop was on
Gestalt Therapy, so it was very fitting that it should be given
in the cabin Fritz Perls, the founder of Gestalt Therapy, had
lived in. This second workshop was led by Jim Simkins and
Robert Reznick, both colleagues of Fritz.

In order for you to understand the significance of my
experiences in this Gestalt workshop, I am going to take
time now to give you some background information on the
nature of Gestalt Therapy and how it is used to bring about
change.

# CHAPTER
# 3

## Gestalt Therapy

One of the most important characteristics of Gestalt Therapy is that it is done totally in the "here and now." Fritz Perls, the founder of Gestalt Therapy, maintains that all therapy can only be done in the now. Anything else is interfering. The best way for a patient to find out what is going on within him is to focus his attention on his "here and now": his posture, the dryness of his throat, the pressure in his chest, his heartbeat, boredom, frustration, anger, and so on. It is by staying in the "here and now" that the patient becomes aware of his "unclosed gestalts," according to Perls, and it is only by becoming aware of his unclosed gestalts that he can close them.

The importance of the foregoing lies in the fact that irrational behavior is the result of long-standing open gestalts; that is, unfinished situations. The gestalt techniques of Perls were developed to help the patient become more fully aware of himself and his unclosed gestalts. A state of awareness is necessary for the discovery and closure of such gestalts. "And I believe that this is the great thing to understand: that awareness per se—by and of itself—can be curative," Perls states.[1]

The word "gestalt" is borrowed from Gestalt Psychology,

in which a gestalt is a configuration consisting of *Ground* (general background) and *Figure* (what the perceiver observes as standing out from the background). In Gestalt Therapy Perls uses the word "gestalt" to refer to a specific kind of relationship between the observer and what he observes in his environment, so that the "figure" in the perceived field is the satisfier of a need. For example, a man is walking along a country road on a hot day and becomes thirsty. He begins to think about water. Suddenly ahead of him he sees a spring. The spring, with water in it, becomes the figure of the gestalt, the need satisfier. The gestalt is the relationship between the observer and the observed water. As long as the person observes the water without drinking it, the gestalt is said to be open. When the person quenches his thirst by drinking the water, the gestalt is said to be closed. Imagine what would happen if this particular gestalt remained unclosed for longer than a certain critical period of time. In the same way, psychologically harmful results are produced by chronically unclosed gestalts in the interpersonal field. An example of this would be a person's never having expressed the resentment he felt toward his father for not listening to him.

The process of discovering long-standing, psychologically critical open gestalts and closing them, or, to put it differently, moving from neurosis to the authentic self, involves going through what Perls describes as the five layers of neurosis. These are the "cliché" layer, the "phony" layer (role playing), the "phobic" layer (avoidance), the "implosive" layer (in which the person finally knows what he wants to do but is immobilized, and in which there is a feeling of deadness), and lastly the "explosive" layer. Once we get in contact with the deadness of the implosive layer and work through the impasse, implosion becomes explosion.[2]

Perls describes four types of explosion, all related to the closing of unclosed gestalts: (1) the explosion into genuine "grief," which may occur in a person who is working through a loss or death that has not been assimilated; (2) the explosion into "anger," which may occur in a person who has repressed long-standing feelings of anger at some key person, such as a mother or a father; (3) the explosion into "joy, laughter, joie de vivre," which may occur in a person as a result of working through critical feelings of anger or grief; and (4) the explosion into "orgasm," which may occur in a person who has been sexually blocked. "These explosions connect with the authentic personality, the true self," Perls states.[3] The life energy which has been bound up in the implosive layer is released and made available for further growth. It should be noted that a single explosion is only a step forward on the road to maturation and not the completed process.

The Gestalt therapist helps the patient to get through the phobic (and other) layers by encouraging him or her to integrate attention and awareness. "Attention," Perls writes, "is a deliberate way of listening to the emerging foreground figure, which in this case is something unpleasant." In working with a patient, the Gestalt therapist acts as a "catalyst by focusing attention on situations in which the patient experiences being stuck—the unpleasantness—and by frustrating his avoidance still further, until he is willing to mobilize his own resources." [4]

Perls emphasizes the importance of working in the "here and now"; yet some unclosed gestalts which require resolution deal with material from the past, such as unresolved attitudes toward parents. Such gestalts can be closed with the help of a special method devised by Perls called the "double-chair technique," in which material from the past is brought into the present in fantasy and dealt with as if it is happening right now. When this method is used, the patient is directed by the therapist to put the person with whom he has unfinished business on one of the chairs in fantasy. He is then told to be whatever age he wants, and to express to this person in the present tense whatever thoughts and feelings he would like. Usually these are ideas and emotions that he has never expressed to this person before.

After he has expressed these feelings to the fantasized person (say, his father), he is asked to sit in the other chair and play the role of his father. When he does this he begins to feel the way he believes his father felt toward him when he was a child.

He is then asked to change chairs again, to play his own role again, and to respond to what he just said. This alternation of roles is continued until the gestalt is closed.

The first feelings to emerge are frequently grief, and then anger, although this sequence may be reversed. After the anger is out, the patient often becomes aware of feelings of love.

It is usual for a patient who has just closed a significant gestalt to say, "I feel lighter. I breathe more easily. I feel clearer. I can think more easily."

You must understand that before entering the Gestalt Workshop at Esalen my experience with it was limited to a small amount of work with George Brown the previous week, although I have studied it extensively since. So on the July morning when I entered Jim Simkins' workshop and looked around with some apprehension, I had very little idea of what was going to happen to me.

I had seen Jim Simkins at meals during the week of my previous workshop, had been introduced to him, and had asked him various questions about Gestalt Therapy, of which I knew almost nothing at that time, and about which I was very curious. Sometimes he didn't answer and just turned away; at other times he grunted a few monosyllabic words, like a Neanderthal man. I was trying to relate to him from my Adapted Child, but he would have none of it.

My feelings were hurt then. Now I would just dismiss him with an internal comment, "Crude bastard." Well, no—not quite, since I have subsequently learned the manipulative intent that underlies superficial questions. You will see how, later.

We all assembled in Fritz's cabin at nine o'clock. When I got there, several men and women were sitting quietly in a large circle. Jim Simkins was in the circle, too. It seemed that the circle radiated out from him. He was a center of energy, solid, substantial, with high-topped, leather, heavy-soled shoes, a red-checked flannel shirt, open at the neck, and a large balding head which I assumed to be full of wisdom; as it turned out, this was the case. The way he dispensed it, however, proved to be surprising. In the end it worked very well for me.

When I entered Fritz's cabin and saw the seminarians and Jim sitting quietly, as if meditating, I was nervous. I had just been through a workshop in which I had learned to feel comfortable, had several exciting experiences, and went a long way in learning to be close, especially with Adeline.

Now I was beginning a new group—twenty-eight people of mixed sexes and ages about whom I knew nothing.

Would they accept me? I will never find another girl like Adeline, I thought—and didn't—not in this workshop. But I did find other things that were invaluable to me.

It was time to start. Jim looked around. "Tell me your names," he said. After everyone had done that he continued with further directions. "Go around the circle and share your expectations and your fears about this workshop."

This produced some concern in those who were novices to the method—like me. Others, old-timers, leapt on the questions like hungry wolves and dispatched them greedily and with satisfaction.

For me it wasn't so easy. I had decided to drop my role as psychoanalyst altogether, and to be receptive to whatever happened. That left me a bit uncertain.

It was my turn. Jim said, "What are your expectations?"

"I'm a psychoanalyst," I announced, falling back on the only thing that I could think of that would give me status (which is just exactly what I had initially decided not to do), "and . . . I'm getting bored with what I'm doing, and I want to learn some new things." Jim said nothing, but nodded his head understandingly. Jim has a very thick neck—he's built like a gladiator—and when he nodded it conveyed a lot of understanding. "What are your fears?" he asked. I started to say I don't know, and stopped, deciding that would be a cop-out. I want to be liked, I thought, but I have just been through an experience showing that I am liked—what's this all about?

"Are you 'rehearsing'?" Jim said. I laughed. "What are you laughing about," Jim said gently. "I guess I'm nervous," I said. "I'm afraid I won't be accepted, liked." That doubt was still there—some of it.

After everyone had given his expectations and fears, Jim said, "Each person pick a partner, preferably of the opposite sex. Get to know your partner without speaking. You can use your hands, eyes, nose—all your senses—and you can make unintelligible noises. Then share your feelings with your partner."

This presented no great problem to me, by this time. The girl next to me, Charlotte, and I sat down on the floor facing each other. I took both of her hands in mine and began to get to know them and her. Although this is an exercise I had already done, it moved me deeply, and seemed like a new experience.

What are your hands like when you begin to get to know another person with them? Are they soft? Are they warm? Are they unhurried? Are they appreciative? Are they sensitive? Are they pliant and resilient? Do they experience the other person as worthwhile? Important?

Or are they tense, hard, insensitive, not in touch with the other person, even though touching her?

Charlotte said, "Your hands are warm and gentle. I like them." I felt the same about Charlotte's hands. Later

Charlotte said, "I thought you needed lots of warmth, so I gave it to you." I didn't like that. I wanted her to be warm to me because she wanted to, and said so. She said, "I know I have a problem with mothering," which helped some. It was important to me that she take the responsibility for *her* problem, and not lay it off on me.

After this exercise was finished, Jim said, "Close your eyes, and go away to any place you want to for about two minutes—then open your eyes and look at us—then go away and then come back again. Then share your feelings with us."

I imagined that I was sitting on a cliff overlooking the Pacific Ocean, watching the large, rolling waves come in slowly and majestically and break on the rocky beach. Then I opened my eyes. Everyone looked the same to me as before.

Then I closed my eyes, and repeated the fantasy trip. Then I opened my eyes again. Everyone still looked the same. I learned later that if a person is anxious to the point where he doesn't see others clearly before he begins this exercise, when he goes away in his fantasy and then opens his eyes and comes back to the group, his psychological vision may become clearer and he may see the others in the group more accurately than he did before.

This didn't happen to me. I guess I wasn't *that* anxious.

"Would you be willing to share your experiences?" Jim asked gently, addressing no one in particular.

Marion said that she had gone in fantasy to a sloop in the Gulf of Mexico, a sloop on which she and a friend had been cruising, and on which she had had many exciting adventures.

After several others described their experiences it was time to close the first day's session.

These exercises may seem simple to you, even trivial. What is there so unusual about telling what you expect from a workshop, and what you fear? The importance is that these questions cannot be answered without getting in touch with feelings. Many people have difficulty in doing this, since in the process of growing up they are taught to repress their feelings. These exercises, and others like them, helped me to recognize and to get in touch with my own feelings again. As a small child I had been in touch with them. Somewhere during the process of growing up I lost them.

The next morning, when the group assembled in Fritz's cabin, Jim started the session by making a few pertinent remarks about Gestalt Therapy which answered some of my questions, some previously verbalized, others unspoken. What he said made a lasting impression on me.

"The 'hanging-on bite,'" he said, "is caused by repressed anger. It is felt physically as a tightening of the jaw muscles. As long as you are angry with someone, you can't let him go. You can't let go, and you can't chew up and digest what you are holding on to, either."

The psychological equivalent of the hanging-on bite is resentment, which Fritz Perls calls "an effort at maintaining the status quo, a hanging-on; in resentment you can neither let go and be done by giving up, nor can you be aggressive and angry and clear up the situation. Resentment is the bite that hangs on."[5] Resentment is an excellent example of an unfinished situation, one in which a person wants to express something but does not; on the contrary, he hangs on to it, so that it is not resolved. This produces feelings of discomfort. Do you remember any situation in your own background, perhaps involving your parents, in which you were angry, but in which you swallowed this anger, did not let it out? This is an unfinished situation, an unclosed gestalt, and this is what leads to the hanging-on bite.

It is important that what was held back originally finally be expressed. Without such expression there can be no real growth.

"I may have to frustrate you," Jim said casually to the group, "in order to mobilize your resentments." This frightened me a bit, since I don't like being frustrated, and at that time the idea of expressing resentments threatened me.

"The question," Jim said, going on with his second statement about the principles of Gestalt Therapy, "is a hook. It is a way of making contact, and not getting very close. Sometimes questions are important, but usually asking questions is a way of trying to get someone else to make a statement for you. 'Aha, I thought, not ever having considered this before, that's why Jim wouldn't answer those questions I asked him last week.

Suddenly Jim looked at me. "You, Richard," he said, "asked questions ad nauseam at first." "Thanks for the 'at first,' " I muttered, still thinking about what Jim said, and wondering how much of my life I had spent trying to get other people to make statements for me. Not owning my own life. That's enough of that, I thought. I'm finished with that. I'm not going to ask any more questions. As a result, to my surprise, I practically stopped talking for a while. I hadn't realized how much of my conversation consisted of asking questions.

Jim continued with a few more general statements about Gestalt. "Never ask 'why,' " he said. "The questions to ask are 'what' and 'how.' 'Why' leads to intellectualizations, to explanations, away from feelings. Change is more likely to occur when a person is in touch with what he or she is actually doing and feeling than when giving an explanation."

Going further, Jim said, "*It* in Gestalt is always *I*. '*It* always happens to me' becomes '*I* always happen to me.' This apparently trivial change in pronouns modifies the whole emphasis of the statement and helps the person who makes the statement to recognize the responsible part he has in it. He becomes more aware that he is not a helpless person in the environment, but an active force, important in his own right.

" 'Take a risk,' is another Gestalt maxim. So is, 'Take

the responsibility.' Both phrases center attention upon the person's own importance in determining his own behavior."

About this time my roommate, Walter, a thirty-two-year-old medical doctor from Honolulu, began smoking a cigar. I don't like cigar smoke, it makes my eyes sting, and then I can't see very well.

I have always been accused of placating the other person, of not saying what I really feel. And several people in encounter groups I had attended had told me that I don't express anger. "Everything you say is nice," a member in such a group once said to me. "I don't trust you."

I decided that next time I would say what I really felt about the cigar smoke and not pull any punches.

The next morning when Walter innocently lit up his cigar I started in. "All that cigar smoke bothers me," I said, speaking from a cloud of smoke that had drifted over to me. "I wish you wouldn't smoke cigars in here." "I like to smoke cigars," Walter replied. "I don't mind as long as I don't have to inhale the smoke," I answered. "The smoke makes my eyes sting and water," I continued, trying to get some feeling into what I said. Walter hung on to his right to smoke a cigar anytime he wanted to. I decided to get really tough. "I wish you would swallow that cigar while it is lighted and that it would burn the hell out of you," I said angrily.

There was no doubt that I let Walter know how I felt. He didn't know that I had used him as a test case to see if I could get out anger when I really felt it, and I did feel it about the billows of smoke that he filled the room with. From that time on, Walter didn't smoke any more cigars in the workshop room.

I had expressed anger and it had worked out fine for me. I had gotten what I wanted. No big deal for most people, perhaps, but for me it was a milestone.

That evening, after the workshop closed, several of us

were walking down to the baths. I was just behind Jim. I had begun to regain some of my confidence by then and was feeling good. Suddenly, in response to an unexpected urge, I said, "Jim, I believe I am going to make it." Jim turned around abruptly and kissed me directly on the lips. To say that I was surprised would be to put it mildly. I wasn't used to such direct expression of feeling without words. I was used to talking "about" feeling, which is much more diluted. This gesture of Jim's left a deep impression upon me. I remember it as vividly as if it had just happened. When Jim gave me that quick, unexpected kiss he was totally in the "now" in the expression of his approval. I will never forget this incident, or the salty taste his lips left upon mine.

An incident occurred in the hot sulfur bath that night that led to dramatic consequences for me. Several of us from the workshop were in the bath together. I was sitting with my back against one side of the bath; the water was about chest high.

Suddenly I felt someone's toes exploring my genitals. I looked up to see whose foot it was. The light was dim, and the bath was crowded, but the foot seemed to come directly from Ralph, a somewhat effeminate-looking man of about thirty.

I was furious, but I didn't say anything about it. In fact the whole thing took me by surprise and for the moment I was taken aback. Before I had time to react further, he pulled his foot away. We are a group that will be using the bath together, I thought, and I don't want to have to wonder whether this will happen again.

The next day, when the group assembled in Fritz's cabin, I decided to describe exactly what happened to me in the bath last night and to say how I felt about it. I looked directly at Ralph and said, "I would like you to keep your foot out of my genitals in the future, because I don't like it." "It wasn't *my* foot," he said. I was angry by then and cried out, "It certainly was. I could tell it was you from the direction your foot came from." "You couldn't see under the water," he said. "There wasn't any other possibility," I replied resentfully. "I could tell it was yours."

This was the whole exchange. Jim didn't make any comment about it. No one in the group said anything about it.

In retrospect, I realize that it might have been an accident, or I could even have been wrong about whose foot it was. No matter, the consequences were the same for me, and they were very important.

From then on I experienced a feeling of being ostracized by the group. In the coffee break no one seemed to want to talk to me. Whatever I said fell flat, and there was little or no response to it from anyone. With Ralph, I couldn't help noticing, things were different. Everyone was talking to him and showing him that they liked him.

I began to feel bad and to withdraw into myself. I began to feel exactly as I had in high school and college: resentful, angry, and introverted. The anger didn't show on the outside. On the surface I was a nice guy. But inside I was boiling. I recognize now that these feelings of internal anger and resentment were exactly like the ones I had about my father, and tried so hard to control by rigid discipline. I had never been able to resolve them in myself, or to work through the intolerable feelings of rejection that I felt as an adolescent. One of the things I had hoped might happen in the workshops at Esalen was that I would work through this unfinished business.

With this in mind, I decided not to be defensive about what was happening to me, but to let it happen (let *I* happen) and see what came out of it (out of *I*).

That afternoon when the group assembled, the pain of feeling rejected was becoming too much to bear. In one of the exercises I was going around the group asking each person for whatever I wanted. I said, "I want you to accept me; I want you to love me." The responses were all noncommittal. One girl, Betty, said: "You are too intellectual. I can't tell what you are feeling. I can't make contact with you." One man, Ernest, turned his back on me and refused to talk.

That did it. I could feel my throat becoming tight. It seemed to be undergoing a kind of spasm quite beyond my ability to control it. It took over, and I lay down on the floor and began to cry convulsively.

I had never been able to cry before—not once during high school years, when I had felt so isolated and hurt and resentful, nor in college, where I had spent most of my time studying and getting high marks and feeling unhappy. I couldn't cry, even though I had thought of committing suicide. I couldn't let out my feelings of despair—or even talk to anyone about them.

But now, in this workshop, as I remembered all this, the floodgates broke. I cried, I sobbed, I lay on the floor, convulsed. There were fourteen people sitting around me in a circle (our large group of twenty-eight had broken up into two subgroups). I wasn't aware of any of them, nor of Bob Reznick, who was leading the group. You could have heard a pin drop. Actually, I wouldn't have heard a thunder clap, I was so deeply immersed in my sorrow and my tears.

In the ten minutes that I lay there sobbing it all came out—the repressed anger and resentment from all those years, the feelings of isolation, the inner turmoil, the agony and the grief. In one tremendous crescendo of pain my sorrow went away. I had let go. I didn't care anymore. I literally didn't care. To hell with the whole goddamn thing, I'm through with it. I'm going to let whoever I am show. I'm going to be "me."

I had begun to let go of the hanging-on bite that I had had for all those lonely years.

After about ten minutes I sat up. My nose was dripping, but I didn't know it till later, when someone gave me some Kleenex.

"Make contact with the group," Bob said. I went to each person, one after the other, and again asked for understanding, acceptance, love. The responses were electrifying to me. Everyone was warm, affectionate, loving.

"I can feel close to you when you show your real feelings," Betty said. Ernest got up from the floor where he was sitting and hugged me.

I can remember exactly the way I felt then. I remember realizing without saying the actual words: It is better to show my feelings and not hold them in. This is what Robert Goulding (more about him later) calls a "redecision," a reversal of the original injunction, "Don't show your feelings," which had played havoc with me for so long.

Once in a while I slip, but for the most part, from that time on, not only have I not withheld my feelings, I haven't even had an inclination to. I *show* my feelings, and I feel good about doing that. Without overdoing it, I actually exult in showing my feelings. It is so different from the way I used to be, and so "refreshing." And everyone likes me better for it, for they know where I am and so they can relate to what is real in me.

As I think about this (for me) extraordinary experience, it is as if I had been changed by a miracle. It wasn't a miracle at all. What happened happened in response to extremely skillfully directed therapy in an environment designed to produce personal growth.

To put it in Fritz Perls' words, I exploded from the "impasse" into grief and freedom and underwent what he would call an organismic change.[6]

The next morning we assembled in Fritz's cabin again. Jim said, "The chair is available." This meant that anyone who wanted to work on a problem could come up and sit in the chair (Perls called it the hot seat) next to him, and he would work with him. There were a few moments of restless silence. I was thinking, I would like to say some things to my father that I have never said before—

unfinished business. I was fearful, hesitating. Suddenly I got up and propelled myself into the chair. My heart was beating hard. This is the way the exchange went:

RICHARD:   My throat is dry and my heart is beating hard.

JIM:   Be your heart.

RICHARD *(I decided to imitate my heart):*   Lub dup, lub dup, lub dup, lub dup, lub dup, lub dup, lub dup, lub dup, lub dup, lub dup. . . . I'm tired of being my heart. I'm going to stop.

JIM:   Is your heart still beating hard?

RICHARD:   No. *(Everyone laughed. I sat quietly for a few moments, uncertain what to say next.)* I want to finish up some unfinished business with my father.

JIM *(looking at me carefully):*   I see a scar on your lips. Would you have a conversation between the scar and your lips.

RICHARD:   There isn't any scar on my lips.

JIM *(still looking closely at my lips):*   I can see one.

I was nonplussed and didn't know what to do, so I sat quietly (in an inner turmoil) for a moment. Then I decided that Jim must be referring to some psychological scar, which there certainly was. I remembered the caption under my photograph in my high school yearbook: "A closed mouth catches no flies." Jim was very perceptive.

Playing both roles, I had the following dialogue with myself:

SCAR:   I am the scar. I am the result of having been badly hurt as a kid by my father not talking to me about anything personal. I am on both lips, and I keep you stuck together, so you can't talk. I am stiff and hard.

LIPS:   We want to break out of this. We don't like to be sealed. We want to open up and speak. We are ashamed. We stay shut and feel angry.

SCAR: I can't help that. I'm the part of you that healed over. You were really hurt by your father, you know. If it weren't for me you would be worse off.

Jim then interrupted.

JIM: Put your father on this chair in fantasy. Be whatever age you want. Call him by the name you called him when he was alive, and tell him in the present tense how you feel about the way he treats you.

RICHARD: I can't do that. I didn't talk to him.

JIM: Tell him that you can't talk to him.

RICHARD: Father, I can't talk to you. You don't listen to me, you don't listen to me. Listen to me, father, listen, LISTEN. AND YOU DON'T TALK TO ME, EITHER.

JIM: Tell your father how you feel when he doesn't talk to you.

RICHARD: I feel left out, alone, angry. Angry, ANGRY. I am going to hit you right on the nose. *(I hit out with my left hand.)*

JIM: Are you left-handed?

RICHARD: *No.* I guess I didn't want to hit him very hard. *(This was a very surprising revelation for me.)* I feel finished. *(I went back to my seat in the circle.)*

This was the beginning but not the end of my attempts to let out my repressed anger at my father.

Although the events I have described were the most significant ones for me, other things also happened to me in this workshop with Jim Simkins:

1. I learned about being in the "here and now." I have experimented with this often after being in the workshop, and have found that when I am in the "here and now" I am not anxious. I am involved in what I am doing, whether it is reading, writing, playing the violin, or admiring the beauty of a woman's face. What I am *doing*

and what I *am* are not separable. I *am* what I am doing and I am doing what I *am.* Anxiety is the space between the "now" and the "then." In the "now" there is no space—only "being." It is amazing how after I learned to be in the "now" anxiety dropped away.

One of the best ways of learning to be in the "now" is to do a hand-to-hand contact with someone you like, or, just as well, with someone you don't know, getting to know his or her hand with your hand, eyes closed and without talking. Exist just in your hand contact, be aware of only that, keep all thoughts out of your head, just be aware of the feelings in your hand. That is the "now" of this experience.

2. I learned not to ask questions in order to get the other person to make a statement. Now I make the statement I had in mind myself. I find this is a more direct and satisfying way of relating, one in which I take charge and assume the responsibility for what I say myself.

3. I learned that the hanging-on bite is no good for anybody. Get out the anger in a fantasy conversation with the person you are angry at, and get it over with. No one can be free to be his or her own self otherwise.

4. I've had a lot of fun with the maxim: *"It is always I."* *"It's* pretty funny" becomes *"I'm* pretty funny." *"It's* too bad it didn't work out" becomes *"I'm* too bad *I* didn't work out." Watch for this *"It* is always *I."* It's dynamite, and blasts away a lot of confusion.

5. "Take a risk." I use this one many times a day. By nature I'm conservative—and that's no way to grow. Take a risk: *It* really helps. *I* really help myself when I do.

6. "Take the responsibility" is another phrase I carry with me and find very useful. "I'll take the responsibility for what I feel and what I do." That makes me feel that I'm in my own power.

7. In this workshop setting I learned that I could express anger at what I didn't like and I would be listened to and taken into account. I say "in the workshop setting"

because I once had a patient who was an account executive in a Madison Avenue advertising agency. Against his inner wishes, he was put in charge of office fire drills. He wanted to refuse the job but couldn't bring himself to. One day there was a drill. Everyone was supposed to leave his office, but the president and a V.I.P. didn't. This angered my patient so much that he dashed into the president's outer office and, overriding a secretary's warning not to disturb the boss because he was in conference, burst into the president's office and ordered him and his visitor to join the other agency employees at a predetermined location. The president refused, whereupon my patient (in his Adapted Child) insisted, without effect.

The next day he told me what happened as an example of how he was learning to assert himself. I was appalled. A few weeks later he was fired. This indiscriminate expression of what he called "self-assertiveness," but what was in reality anger at authority figures, is obviously unwise. Feelings should be expressed in an appropriate setting.

8. One of the most important things I learned is that I am liked better if I show how I really feel.

After I got home from Esalen things were never quite the same for me again. To begin with, I looked at Corlis differently. The night I arrived, she met me at the door. I looked at her "eye to eye." "You never looked at me that way before," she said. "I really feel taken in." I *was* "seeing" her in a way I never had before, and it *(I)* made me feel good that she noticed it *(I)*.

When I went back to work in my office in New York I introduced the exercises that I learned at Esalen to my therapy groups. I had three ongoing groups at the time. We did "eye-to-eye contact," "getting to know the other person's hand with your eyes closed and without talking," "the blind walk," and others.

For my patients these were entirely new experiences.

The members of the groups became deeply involved with them, as I had. The "permission" to be close implied in these exercises affected them deeply, as it had me. "Permission to be close," please note; not permission to have sex.

Being close has a value for me now that is different from before. Now I can be in contact by touch without feeling nervous about it, because I am not making a sexual overture. I am communicating in a medium different from words, a more direct and less confusing medium. In words I can say, "I love you" when I really hate you and want to spit in your face, and you may be deceived for the moment. But not when I communicate with touch. Touch is a more primary way of communicating: deeper, more elemental, more immediate, more direct—and more satisfying.

Here rested my personal odyssey into change for a year—at least the traveling part—but I kept changing, because I applied what I had learned at Esalen in my everyday life and in my practice.

It turned out to be extremely effective in helping patients to overcome deep conflicts, and the effects were more rapid and profound than when I used psychoanalytic techniques alone.

I remember one extraordinary case of rapid change in a patient. I say extraordinary because prior to my going to Esalen such a change would have taken much longer. Using the methods that I had learned at Esalen, a dramatic change occurred within two sessions.

This was the case of a thirty-year-old married woman, Ruth, the wife of a physician. She had a six-month-old child, a healthy, active little boy. She was hysterical in her fear that her child, when crawling about on the rug, would swallow a pin or some other sharp object that she had failed to pick up when cleaning the rug, and that this would seriously injure him.

Her husband had tried to reassure her by discussion and persuasion prior to her coming into therapy—all to no avail.

When I first saw her, the pressure of her anxiety was tremendous, and she talked so fast that I could hardly understand her. After questioning her about her problems and talking with her about them—with no effect whatsoever—I suggested that her anxiety might be diminished if she would learn to be in the "here and now." I explained to her that her fear was of something that she was afraid would happen in the future, and not something that was happening "now." I said that if she would be in the "now," she would be involved with doing something "now," and what she was doing would take the place of her fear.

A Freudian analyst might have interpreted her fear as a defense against her unconscious desire to kill her own child. This would have been placing ideas in her head that she didn't have at all. It is what Fritz Perls would call "mind-fucking." Since, as it turned out, this was obviously not true (but just the reverse), it would have had the result of setting her off in the wrong direction. She could have continued to work on it five times a week for several years without changing, except possibly for the worse.

The actual fact was that she was in her Adapted Child, to use Transactional Analysis language (see Chapter Four), and under the influence of the negative messages (Tapes) which she had received from her mother, namely, "You will never do anything right, and you will not make a good mother." This is what she was anxious about.

She really hated the Adapted Child in herself, which I helped her to modify later. At the moment I was more concerned with helping her to diminish her anxiety.

I helped her to learn how to be in the "here and now" toward the end of the first session by doing a "hand-to-hand contact" with her and specifically directing her to keep all thoughts out of her head and to concentrate only on the contact with my hand and the response that it evoked in her hand.

She did this successfully and reported that she felt a sudden, unexpected sense of peace.

At the beginning of the second session she told me that after her first session she had walked through Central Park and had experienced a sense of clarity that she had not had for many months.

In this second session I continued with the general theme of keeping in the "here and now." One effective way of doing this, which I had learned at Esalen, is massage. I gave her a massage, directing her to be aware only of the touch of my hands and the feelings they evoked in her. She did this, and during this session her anxiety went away. She felt lighter, she breathed more easily, her face dropped the tense, anxious look that she had had before starting therapy, and she expressed deep feelings of relief.

At the time I was thinking only of the effect of these exercises in helping her to get into the "here and now," but in retrospect I see that I was also giving her "unconditional stroking" (a TA term for unconditional acceptance)—the kind of unconditional acceptance she had always wanted as a child. This helped her to accept her own internal Child, a subject that was dealt with in detail as her therapy progressed. But in two sessions, Ruth's anxiety had diminished from an excessive amount, which continually pressured her, to practically none.

This didn't mean that she was "cured" in just two sessions. She wasn't. However, by learning to be in the "here and now," and using it as a general principle of living every day, she became able to secure almost immediate relief from her anxiety, so that she was able to work through her problems in therapy much more quickly than would otherwise have been the case. In only six months by mutual decision, we terminated this successful therapy.

As one by-product of applying the "here and now" principle in all aspects of her life, sexual relationships with her husband improved immensely. Prior to therapy she had stopped having intercourse with him. Now she resumed and enjoyed it.

Three months after terminating therapy Ruth dropped in to see me and told me that she was no longer worried about pins on the carpet. She said she had a feeling of well-being such as she had never enjoyed before.

# CHAPTER
# 4

## Transactional Analysis
## —A Key to
## Self-understanding

The nonverbal and Gestalt experiences I had at Esalen were invaluable both for my personal growth and for my work with patients. About a year later, at a dinner party at the New Orleans meeting of the American Group Psychotherapy Association, I learned about Transactional Analysis from Dr. Robert Goulding and Mary Edwards Goulding. Dr. Goulding told me that he combined Transactional Analysis with Gestalt Therapy, and felt the results were better than with Gestalt Therapy alone. He was thoroughly familiar with the principles of Gestalt Therapy and had been a co-therapist with Fritz Perls in workshops at Esalen and elsewhere.

I asked him to tell me about Transactional Analysis, which he did briefly. He invited me to attend a workshop with him and Mary at the Western Institute for Group and Family Therapy in Watsonville, California. I accepted.

Before I went to the Western Institute I knew very little about Transactional Analysis (TA). Since going there I have attended many workshops in TA, have led many myself, have read most of the books in the field, and have become a Teaching Member of the International Transactional Analysis Association.

In order for you to understand better what happened to me, and what went on in the workshop I attended with Bob and Mary Goulding, I am now going to summarize the basic principles of TA.

If you are already familiar with these principles, you may wish to skip on to Chapter Five. My intention here is to provide a concise primer, or mini-reference guide, for those unacquainted with TA and those who wish to refresh their memory. However, I have also included summaries of some of the newer TA concepts (the miniscript, symbiosis, and discounting) because I am convinced of their therapeutic usefulness.

If you will read this carefully, I believe you will find it helpful in evaluating your own life, deciding whether you want to change it, and how you can accomplish this if you do. As a matter of fact, you will know a great deal more about TA than I did that morning when I entered Bob and Mary's living room for that first, for me, epoch-making TA workshop.

Transactional Analysis is a system for understanding the human personality and a method of therapy for correcting its deviations and facilitating personal growth. It has a simplified, easily understandable vocabulary consisting of fifteen key words or concepts. These are: Strokes, Parent, Adult, Child, Transactions, Injunctions, Counterinjunctions, Early Decision, Script, Counterscript, Games, Rackets, Stamps, Redecision, and Contracts.

If you understand these key words and concepts you will be in possession of a great deal of information that will help you understand yourself better.

When I say this, I am writing from my own experience, because for me TA brought together many divergent concepts that I already knew in a way that made them more useful to me in therapy, and in addition added several new and exciting ones.

And I found it invaluable for gaining further understanding of myself, which was essential for the change I was seeking so urgently.

## I. STROKES

Transactional Analysis was developed by Eric Berne, who, as noted previously, was a medical doctor and psychiatrist with psychoanalytic training. His mother was an editor and his father a doctor. It is not surprising, therefore, that he became a writer as well as a therapist interested in curing people.

Dr. Berne was particularly impressed with the importance of strokes. Strokes are the TA unit of recognition. Berne says starkly that without strokes the spinal cord shrivels up. This is true, for nerve cells need stimulation, and without it their tiny processes begin to retract.

Infants who are not sufficiently stroked, as in foundling homes of the last century, became retarded. Some become schizophrenic. Some die. The importance of strokes cannot be overestimated.

Strokes may be nonverbal or verbal. The first strokes that an infant receives are nonverbal ones. Such strokes are given by the doctor when the infant emerges from the birth canal.

The mother holds and cuddles and nurses the infant—all life-giving strokes given before the infant understands the meaning of words, or, in fact, the meaning of anything. Almost everything a mother does to or with her child is a stroke, either positive or negative. At first strokes are given by touch—positive when the touch is gentle, caressing and soothing; negative when it is rough. I once saw a schizophrenic mother who had just finished nursing her baby drop him a distance of one foot into his crib—a negative stroke.

A mother gives strokes also by sounds—cooing, singing,

and by the pleasant, gentle, affectionate, and reassuring tone of her voice as she talks to her child. These are positive strokes. If she yells, or if the sound of her voice is strident and angry, the stroking is negative. She also gives strokes by her facial expression and gestures, and body language. When she smiles at her child this is a positive stroke; when she grimaces at him angrily, it's a negative stroke.

As the child grows older and begins to understand words, mother strokes him verbally. "I love you" is a positive stroke. "I can't stand you" is a negative stroke.

An important thing to understand is that words are symbols for something else. They are not that something else. Thus a mother who has an unwanted child may say to him (out of a sense of guilt) "I love you" when in fact she doesn't love him at all—she hates him. Stroking words have stroking value only when they are invested with the emotion they are intended to express.

Although much of the stroking that occurs in our culture is verbal, since there is a general taboo on touching, words are dependable sources of strokes only when the sound of the voice, the facial expression, and the body language are consonant. Touching, tone of voice, facial expression, and body language are more easily recognized for what they are. I have found that nonverbal ways of communicating are especially valuable in therapy.

I don't intend to underplay the real and significant value of words as sources of strokes. When given honestly and forthrightly, with a sense of integrity, they are very powerful sources of strokes, either positive or negative.

There are four kinds of strokes: (1) *Positive unconditional* strokes, as when a mother says to her child in one way or another, "I love you just for being." (2) *Positive conditional* strokes, as when a mother says, "I will love you if you get high marks in school. (3) *Negative conditional,* as when the mother says to her little girl, "I am going to spank you if you spill the milk." (4) *Negative unconditional,* as when the mother says to her child, "You are just a nuisance, get lost."

The best strokes are positive unconditional and positive conditional; that is, recognition for being and recognition for doing.

The worst strokes are negative unconditional strokes, such as "I can't stand the sight of you."

The most terrible thing of all is to get no strokes. This situation is intolerable, and when it occurs people often set up situations so that they get negative strokes, because negative strokes are better than no strokes. This is seen very early in life, as with children who spill their milk just to get mother's attention. They would rather be yelled at and spanked than ignored.

In fact, rather than go without any strokes, a person may hit himself and thus give himself a stroke. I had a patient who told me that as a child no attention at all was paid to her at the dinner table. After dinner she would hit herself on the head so she would feel alive. She had no idea why she did this. She was giving herself strokes.

Positive physical strokes are holding hands, caressing, hugging (in a friendly way or a sexy way), kissing, touching. Positive verbal strokes can be about the way a person looks or smiles or moves, about his or her body, posture, manner of speech or tone of voice, about his or her personality or accomplishments.

Strokes are the most important psychological events in our lives. The attitude that you and I had about ourselves when we were children [1] was determined by the kinds of strokes we received.

Thus a child reacts to the right combination of positive unconditional and positive conditional strokes with a feeling of "I'm OK–You're OK." Such a child will probably be a winner. As the number of positive strokes decreases and the number of negative strokes increases, the child's existential position becomes "I'm not OK–You're OK." When the number of negative strokes a child receives is overwhelmingly great, his position may become "I'm OK–You're not OK," or in more severe cases, "I'm not

OK—You're not OK." Such children will probably become losers, or even criminals.

Once these positions are established in a person's childhood they are difficult to alter and usually stay with him into adulthood and significantly affect his life behavior. However, they are usually modifiable in therapy.

Because of the rules about giving and receiving strokes, in large numbers of families and in our culture in general, many people live under a stroke deficit.

Transactional Analysis stresses the importance of learning to get and to give strokes.

## II. EGO STATES: PARENT, ADULT, CHILD

Eric Berne's ideas and theories grew out of his work with patients. He was a keen observer and an acute listener. As he worked with patients, he observed that their behavior would change abruptly from time to time in ways that puzzled him. At one time a patient would be talking exactly as one of his or her parents did; at another time he or she would be feeling and acting like a child. At still other times the patient would be straightforward and factual and appraise his or her problems realistically.

From these and other observations Dr. Berne concluded that not only his patients, but all of us, think, feel, act, talk, and respond from three basic positions which he called *ego states.*

Berne describes ego states as "coherent systems of thought and feeling manifested by corresponding patterns of behavior." [2]

Our personality, Berne says, is composed of three ego states, which he calls Parent, spelled with a capital P to distinguish it from our real parents; Adult, spelled with a capital A to distinguish it from the adult person; and Child, spelled with a capital C to distinguish it from the real child that we once were.

Figure 1 is a structural diagram of the human personality, showing the ego states. The line surrounding all of
them is the envelope corresponding to the rest of the body.
In actual practice this envelope is not usually drawn. When
it is not, the diagram is called an informal structural
diagram, as in Figure 2.

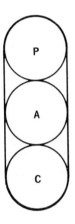

Figure 1. Formal Structural Diagram

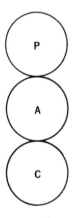

Figure 2. Informal Structural Diagram

*Parent.* The Parent is that part of our personality which consists of the messages and slogans that we received from our own parents when we were children. These messages are colloquially called "parental tapes" because as we go through our lives we keep replaying them, like tapes from a tape recorder. When we express them, they may be directed at ourselves or other people in our environment.

Here are some of the parental messages I have heard from my patients: "Work hard and be a credit to your family." "It's important to be head of the class." "You don't go to school for fun, you go there to work." "Look both ways before you cross the street." "Always wear your rubbers when it rains." "Don't talk to strangers." "The worst thing is to be poor." "Love of money is the root of all evil." "Don't leave any food on the plate." "Keep smiling." "Always think of others."

Some parental slogans are based on prejudices—for example, the discounting of persons of other races, nationalities, religions, politics, or occupations. The child who has received such parental prejudices grows up with these stereotypes in his own Parent and doesn't see the real person, unless he begins to do some processing through his Adult.

Some Parent directives are constructive and even life-saving in a crisis, when there is no time to think. For instance, "Look both ways before you cross the street" has become reflex with me and is particularly useful in New York traffic.

Parental directives are important in making it possible not to have to process every event, since parental messages deal with what to do and what not to do, what is good and what is bad, and how to live your life. Many of them are OK.

Of course, in this rapidly changing society of ours, many parental slogans may be out of date, since, if we are adults, the ones that constitute our Parent ego state were given to us many years ago.

If you have children of your own, have you ever been startled to hear one of them echoing something you have said in exactly the same tone of voice, such as, "Money doesn't grow on trees, you know." She is speaking from her Parent ego state. Or you may hear your neighbor's little boy saying confidentially to your child, "All politicians are crooks." He is in his Parent ego state and is reflecting his parents' attitudes.

Neither child has any conception of money or politics. Such parental slogans are recorded in the brain of the child and are accepted as fact. They fire off repeatedly throughout life and significantly affect the person's behavior.

The Parent ego state is divided into the Nurturing Parent and the Critical, or Prejudicial, Parent.*

When a mother hugs her little girl and says, "I love you," she is in her Nurturing Parent; if she says to her angrily, "Why are you so stupid and clumsy?" she is in her Critical Parent.

The Nurturing and Critical aspects of the Parent ego state are indicated as shown in Figure 3.

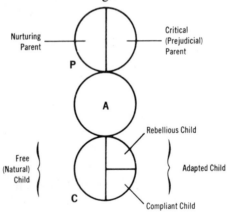

Figure 3. Descriptive Aspects of the Personality

* *Prejudicial* was the term first selected by Eric Berne. In his last book he changed *Prejudicial* to *Critical*. Some writers prefer one and some the other; in this book they are used interchangeably.

The *Nurturing Parent* ego state may be further sub-divided into an OK part and a Not-OK part. The *OK Nurturing Parent* says such things as, "I love you just as you are, just because you are you," and, "I'm proud of you for doing so well in the test you took yesterday." The Nurturing Parent gives *permission* and *protection*. These may be directed internally to the person's own Child or Adult, or externally, to the Parent, Adult and Child of others.

When a person is in his OK Nurturing Parent his voice will usually be warm, comforting, nurturing, and his facial expression and bodily posture relaxed, open and accepting.

The *Not-OK Nurturing Parent* says such things as, "I'll do that for you," to a person who wants to do it for himself. The Not-OK Nurturing Parent is overprotective, enveloping, engulfing. A father who insists on fixing his son's bicycle when his son would rather fix it himself is in his Not-OK Nurturing Parent. The Not-OK Parent gives crooked positive strokes. The strokes are crooked because they are given to satisfy an irrational need in the Not-OK Nurturing Parent. They do not increase the self-esteem of the person to whom they are given; they weaken it.

The Not-OK Nurturing Parent enters the Karpman Drama Triangle as a rescuer (see p. 85), and frequently ends up as a victim of the person it is overprotecting, who may ultimately revolt, as in the case of children of overprotective parents who ultimately insist upon their own autonomy.

The *Critical Parent* may likewise be subdivided into two parts: the *OK Critical Parent* and the *Not-OK Critical Parent*. The *OK Critical Parent* says such things as, "Don't drive your car around a sharp curve when going sixty miles an hour." The OK Critical Parent criticizes constructively, both when the criticisms are directed internally, at oneself, and externally, at others.

The *Not-OK Critical Parent* says such things as, "Can't you do anything right? You're so stupid. Get lost." The Not-OK Critical Parent's criticisms come out of a need to discount, and are unjustified.

*Adult.* The Adult ego state works like a computer. Berne states, "It appraises its environment and calculates its possibilities and probabilities." [3] It works out options. It is the part of the personality which deals with the facts. It does not have emotions. This does not mean that emotions are bad. It means that the Adult works best when it is not affected or swayed by feelings.

When you multiply 10 by 20 and come up with the answer 200, you are in your Adult.

When the Adult receives and stores accurate information, its answers are usually better than Parent ego state answers, since the facts fed into it are usually more up-to-date.

*Child.* Just as each person carries around within himself a parent, so, according to Berne, "each person carries within himself a little boy or little girl, who feels, thinks, acts, talks, and responds just the way he or she did when he or she was a child of a certain age." [4]

There are two aspects to the Child ego state. These are: the Free, or Natural Child * (Prince or Princess), and the Adapted Child (Frog). The Adapted Child, in turn, may be either Compliant or Rebellious.

The Free Child is spontaneous, loving or hateful, outgoing, impulsive, playful, creative, and autonomous. The Adapted Child (Compliant part) is unduly concerned with how others feel about him or her, and with pleasing others, is guilty, ashamed, fearful. The Rebellious part of the Adapted Child is angry and resentful.

A man who walks out of the front door whistling, with a set of golf clubs over his shoulder, is in his Free Child. So is the woman whose eyes are shining as she puts on her new lynx fur coat and smiles at herself in the mirror.

A man who wants to invite a woman that he met at a cocktail party to have dinner and go to the ballet with him,

---

* The terms "Free Child" and "Natural Child" are used interchangeably in TA literature.

but is afraid to for fear she might not accept, is in his Compliant Adapted Child.

The college student who says to his roommate, "Nobody can make me study" is in his Rebellious Adapted Child.

Each of these divisions of the Child ego state is further divided into two parts, an OK part and a Not-OK part.

The *OK Free Child* says such things as, "Wow, I had a great time at the party!" The OK Free Child is spontaneous, loving, outgoing, impulsive, fun loving, creative and autonomous, all within realistic limits. The OK Free Child processes its impulses through the Adult ego state.

*The Not-OK Free Child* approves of such things as getting into a car without having first learned how to drive it and starting off for the thrill of it. The Not-OK Free Child is impulsive and does things without first processing them through the Adult. A person following his Not-OK Free Child impulses often ends up disasterously.

The *OK Compliant Child* is compliant when necessity demands it. The capacity to adapt, and to follow the directions given by the president of the company that employs you, may be essential if you wish to continue in its employ. The adaptiveness of the OK Compliant Child may in some circumstances even be essential to survival, as in the case of Naomi, a Jewish girl who was forced to go into hiding in Nazi occupied Belgium (see Chapter 7).

The *Not-OK Compliant Child* is compliant when there is no necessity to be so. Usually the Not-OK Compliant Child results from the child making a decision early in life to follow the irrational messages (injunctions and counterscript drivers, see Chapter 4, p. 92 and p. 101) given to him by his parents. Thus, the child whose father says, "Get out of the way or I'll knock your head off," decides to get out of his way. This makes sense at the time. However, when the child grows up to be a man, and his father has died, if he continues to react to others as if he has to get out of their way or they will knock his head off, then he is acting out of his Not-OK Compliant Child. He does not see others as they really are, but as his father was, and so reacts to them inappropriately. He tries too hard to please others, he hesitates to say what he really thinks and feels. On the contrary, he is continually making an effort to figure out what others want him to say; consequently it is difficult to get to know who he really "is." The Not-OK Compliant Child is usually shy and withdrawn, and lacks the capacity for healthy intimacy.

The *OK Rebellious Child* rebels when there is something real to rebel against. Thus, when parents are unrealistic in their demands, the OK Rebellious Child of the child rebels. The same reaction may occur in adults, as in the case of George Washington, Thomas Jefferson, Benjamin Franklin, and the other Founding Fathers of our country. Patrick Henry's battle cry, "Give me liberty or give me death," is the response of his OK Rebellious Child to oppression.

The *Not-OK Rebellious Child* says such things as, "No, I won't do what you want me to," even when this is reasonable and actually important to his own welfare. The Not-OK Rebellious Child behaves as if the only satisfactory answer is "no," when someone, particularly an authority figure, asks him to do something. He rebels for the sake of rebelling, and not for a real cause. The Not-OK Rebellious Child is Adapted because he lacks autonomy. He may feel that his Not-OK rebellion gives him freedom, but it does not. His reactions depend upon others toward whom he responds with spitefulness and anger.

Second-order structural analysis shows that the Child ego state of a child also contains a Parent, Adult, and Child, as shown in Figure 4.

The Parent ego state of the Child of the child is called the Electrode—the point of fixation in the Child of the negative messages from the Child of the parent. The Adult ego state of the Child of the child is called the Little Professor; it acts intuitively in the interest of survival on the basis of limited information. The Child ego state of the child is called the Demon—the source of basic instinctual drives and impulses.

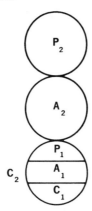

Figure 4. Second Order Structural Analysis

(Despite the connotations of Eric Berne's term, the Demon can also be thought of as everything in the child which does not come from an outside source, that is inherent or intrinsic.)

When the Adult ego state takes in and stores incorrect information which originates in the Parent or Child, this is called a *contamination.* When such contamination is from the Parent, it is called a prejudice, as in the case of a person who thinks it is sinful to dance. When such contamination is from the Child, it is called a delusion, as in the case of a woman who believes that someone is watching her get undressed even when the door is closed and the shades are down, so no one can look in; or the patient in a hospital who sees call numbers of the doctors flashing on the screen and believes that someone from outside the hospital is flashing a message to him.

Figure 5 illustrates such contamination, the contamination in this case being double.

One important aspect of therapy is decontamination of the Adult. This is illustrated in Figure 6.

Of the three ego states only two, the Parent and Child, have feelings. The Child is considered, in TA, to be the origin of what is best in our personalities, since from it come

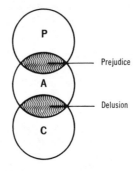

Figure 5.  Contamination of the Adult ego state by material from the Child and the Parent (double contamination)

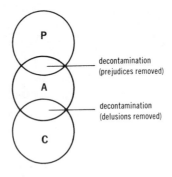

Figure 6.  Decontamination

autonomy, creativity, pleasure in living, and reproduction. Through the activities of the Child we renew ourselves.

When one ego state is in control, it is said to be in the *executive,* and when it continues to be in control so that the other two ego states are excluded, it is said to be *excluding.*

In the healthy person all of the ego states are available and there is a continuous process of checking and counter-checking between them.

Without the help of the Nurturing Parent and Adult, the Child would soon end up in trouble, since it is characteristic of the Child ego state that "it wants what it wants when it wants it."

The person who is exclusively in his Adult soon finds life to be dull and uninteresting.

The person who is in his excluding Parent is always telling someone else what to do, rather than living his own life.

Ego states can be recognized in three ways: first, by the person's use of certain key words; second, by the tone and quality of the voice; and third, by the facial expression and bodily postures.

Key Parent words are *do, don't, should, shouldn't, must, mustn't, have to, ought to,* and sometimes *never* and *always.*

*"Do* your homework, Herbert," is from the Parent ego state. So is, *"Don't* play with matches," "You *should* be quiet when your father comes home," "You *shouldn't* make so much noise," "You *must* go to visit your Aunt Sally," "You *have to* go to bed by nine o'clock," "You *ought to* eat your salad, Raymond," *"Never* do that again," and "You *always* come home late."

Whether the Parent ego state is Nurturing or Critical cannot always be determined by the key Parent words, since any one of them might be used in both of these aspects. For example, the simple statement, "Do your homework, Herbert," is from the Nurturing Parent if it is said in a pleasant tone of voice, with the child's interest at heart; it is from the Critical Parent if it is said in an angry or resentful fashion, as if the parent is finding a convenient way to vent his hostility.

A Nurturing Parent facial expression is warm and affectionate; a Critical Parent facial expression is hard, set, angry, and reproving.

A typical Parent gesture is pointing the finger at the person you are talking to.

Words characteristic of the Adult ego state are "factual" words, not "feeling" words, and the tone of voice is factual and level-headed. Similarly, the facial expression is serious, as when a person is working out a problem which requires his complete attention. The body posture is congruent with this; for example, the head is held straight.

Key words for recognizing the Child ego state are: *wish, want, try, because, can't, won't,* and such phrases as: "I wish I could," "I'm afraid," "I'll try," "I can't" (Adapted Child), and "That's great," and "Wow!" (Free Child).

The facial expression of the person who is in his Free Child ego state is open, outgoing, warm, trusting, friendly, happy. His bodily gestures go along with this and are open and unconstrained.

The facial expression of the person who is in his Adapted Child ego state is tentative or withdrawn or sulking or frightened. His bodily movements and gestures and postures may be either tentative and constrained or loose, floppy, and uncontrolled.

The facial expression of the Rebellious Child is angry and resentful. His movements are aggressive, and his bodily postures tense.

The Free Child voice is joyous; the Adapted Child (Compliant part) is weak, whining, complaining, compliant; the Rebellious Child voice is angry.

Child gestures are: looking up, or sideways, or tilting the head.

Here are some examples that may help you to learn to identify ego states:

The boy walked down the street whistling "Yankee Doodle Dandy" (Free Child).

Johnny looked at Sara (his older sister) and complained in a whining voice, "You never give me anything" (Adapted Child).

Mother calls to Joe, her six-year-old son, who is playing on the beach, "We have to leave this very minute." Her voice is critical and demanding (Critical Parent).

Joe responds by yelling angrily, "I'm going for another swim," whereupon he jumps up and dashes into the ocean (Adapted Child, Rebellious part).

A mother is talking to her sixteen-year-old daughter, who has just played the leading role in a high school play. "Mary," she says in a warm and interested and approving voice, "I was so proud of you when I saw you in the play last night. You were a perfect princess" (Nurturing Parent).

Mother, speaking to her twelve-year-old daughter: "It's too bad you look like your father. He's the ugly one in the family, you know. I don't know why you couldn't have taken after my side of the family" (Critical Parent).

Mother, speaking to her daughter who is a junior in high school: "Mary, your father and I will send you to college, since you want to go so much. But you will never graduate. You are so stupid" (Critical Parent).

Husband, speaking seriously to wife: "Maude, I've gone over our bank account, and we have enough money saved up to make that trip around the world. I'm crazy to go, how about you?"(Adult ego state when assessing the bank account; this shifts to Free Child).

## III. TRANSACTIONS: COMPLEMENTARY, CROSSED, AND ULTERIOR

In order to understand how you relate to other people, it is necessary to understand the character, or types, of your transactions with them.

A transaction is the TA unit of communication. It consists of a stimulus from one of the ego states of an Agent to one of the ego states of a Respondent, and a response from the Respondent to one of the ego states of the Agent.

There are three kinds of transactions: complementary, crossed, and ulterior.

1. *Complementary transaction.* If you ask a friend what time it is, and he responds with the answer, "Seven o'clock," that is a complementary or uncrossed transaction. It is diagramed as shown below in Figure 7, and you will see that the arrows do not cross.

In a complementary transaction the response comes from the *same* ego state in the Respondent to which the stimulus was directed and is returned to the *same* ego state in the Agent that initiated the transaction. Complementary transactions can be continued without interruption.

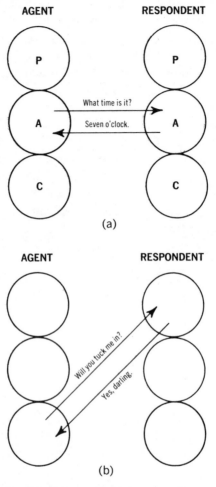

Figure 7.  Complementary (uncrossed) Transactions

2. *Crossed transaction.* Suppose you ask your friend "What time is it?" and he replies, angrily, "You're always worrying about what time it is. Who cares?" This is a crossed transaction. In a crossed transaction the response comes from a *different* ego state than the one to which the stimulus was directed.

You will see that the stimulus question is Adult to Adult,

but the response is Child to Parent. Your question hooked his Rebellious Child, and in his response he attacked your Parent.

Since you have done nothing to provoke this response, it is irrational. In psychoanalysis, such a response is called a "transference reaction."

Once a transaction has become crossed, like this one, there is nowhere to go with it, and communication stops until the person who made the irrational response returns to his Adult ego state. What usually happens is that a fight occurs, with resultant bad feelings.

Figure 8 illustrates this crossed transaction.

3. *Ulterior transaction.* An ulterior transaction contains a hidden message. It is intended to influence the Respondent without his or her being aware of it. Ulterior transactions are the currency of the con artist. They are the basis for transactional analysis games.

In an ulterior transaction the spoken message is addressed to one ego state whereas the unspoken message is addressed to a different ego state in order to elicit a desired response. This can involve three ego states in an angular transaction (Fig. 9a) or four ego states in a duplex transaction (Fig. 9b).

The following are examples of ulterior transactions (see Fig. 9).

A salesman knocks on the door and asks the housewife if she would like to buy a set of pots and pans. She says, "Yes" and asks him to show her what he has. He does, and then says, "This is the best set, but it's very expensive." His ulterior message (which is unspoken) is, "You're too poor to buy it." This hooks her Adapted Child and she says, "That's the one I'll take."

A man approaches a woman at a party and says to her, "Would you like to take a walk on the beach? It's such a nice night." His ulterior message, from his Free Child and perhaps reinforced with nonverbal signals, is "Let's have some sex." The woman replies from her Adult, "I would be happy to" (walk on the beach), at the same time responding

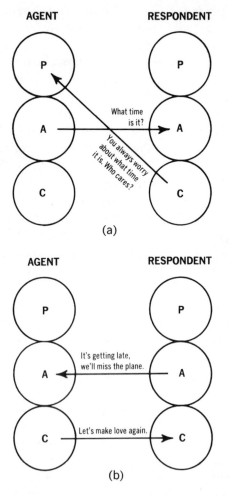

Figure 8.   Crossed Transactions

from *her* Free Child with the ulterior message, "Let's"
(have some sex).

## *Options*

Have you ever been in the situation where, for example,
another person has been critical of you (coming from her/
his Prejudicial, or Critical, Parent) and you were trying to

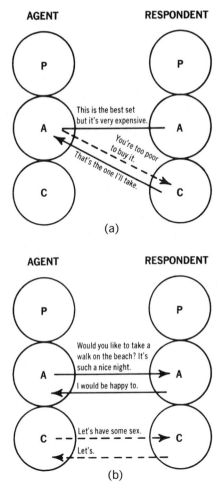

Figure 9. Ulterior Transactions

win her/his approval by responding with explanations (from your Adapted Child), only to find out that you were locked in a Prejudicial Parent–Adapted Child dialogue, which solved nothing? No matter how many explanations you gave, you were unable to terminate this.

Stephen Karpman has developed an interesting and useful way of interrupting such "locked" transactions.[5] This can be done, he says, by the person who is criticized

(Respondent) responding from a different ego state in herself/himself, or addressing a different ego state in the other person (Agent, or Initiator). In this way the original transaction is crossed and the subject is changed. Karpman says that there are twenty-four ways of crossing a transaction, and thus unlocking the "locked" dialogue, each one separate and discrete from the other, but in the following examples I will show only three.

Just before leaving for a party, Jack says, with irritation, to his wife, Judy, "You are never ready on time." Judy responds by saying, "I had to put the children to bed." Her husband replies, "You always have some excuse." The conversation continues in this vein for several minutes and becomes more heated. Judy wants to terminate it but can't think of a way to get out of it. Furthermore, this happens repeatedly, and she is sick of this whole subject. In addition, she and her husband never are actually late for parties.

The transactions given above can be illustrated with the help of Figure 10.

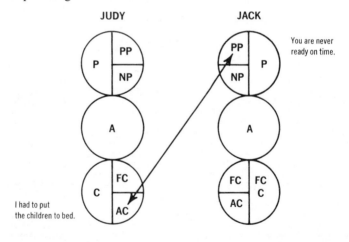

Figure 10. Options Diagram

Jack's original criticism comes from his Prejudicial Parent and is addressed to Judy's Adapted Child. Judy replies with an excuse from her Adapted Child, as shown in the diagram. She can cross these PP–AC transactions in any one of the three following ways:

1. She can shift from her Adapted Child to her Prejudicial Parent while still continuing to address Jack's Prejudicial Parent. The following remark from July illustrates this: PP–PP: "I didn't know I was married to a metronome."

2. She can shift from her Adapted Child to her Adult, and address Jack's Adult: A–A: "You're so right. Let's find a quiet time to talk this over."

3. She can shift from her Adapted Child to her Free Child, and address Jack's Free Child: FC–FC: "Hey, you look great in that jacket."

Using Options is a fascinating way to learn to control all your ego states and to become aware of what ego state the other person is coming from when transacting with you.

Becoming familiar with the concept of options shows you, as Karpman says, that there are such options, that they can be used to solve immediate problems, and that through them you can discover the permissions you need to give yourself to use them. Options also show you that you have a right to demand straight transactions, to protect yourself, to express yourself, to see that others are using options, to see ego states correctly in others, and to use all your ego states. Using options will, in addition, help you to discover your childhood prohibitions.

If you are interested in learning more about options and how to use them, refer to Karpman's original article. This material has not, so far as I am aware, been published in book form, but the article can be purchased from ITAA Publications, 1772 Vallejo Street, San Francisco, California 94123.

## IV. THE DUSAY EGOGRAM

Dr. John Dusay developed a bar-gram system which I have found extremely useful. Called an *egogram,* it shows graphically the amount of energy in each ego state of the personality. It is based on the assumption that 100 percent of the psychic energy is invested in the ego states, and that whatever is invested in one cannot be invested in another. This means that if there is a change in the energy content of one (for instance, the Prejudicial Parent or the Adapted Child) there must be a change in the energy content of one or more of the other ego states.[6] This is illustrated in Figures 11 and 12.

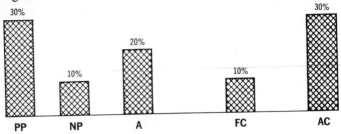

Figure 11. Egogram showing a person with a highly developed Prejudicial Parent (PP) ego state and a correspondingly high Adapted Child (AC). Nurturing Parent (NP) and Free Child (FC) are low. Adult (A) is moderately developed.

Another means of expressing the same concept is the personality formula. Using the percentage of energy in each ego state as an indication of the strength of each ego state, the personality formula for the person illustrated in Figure 11 would be PP [30], NP [10], A [20], FC [10], AC [30]. During the process of therapy this changed to PP [6], NP [30], A[28], FC [30], AC [6], as shown in Figure 12.

You can learn a great deal about yourself by drawing your own egogram. It is a surprisingly effective exercise in getting to know yourself better, and I suggest that you try it.

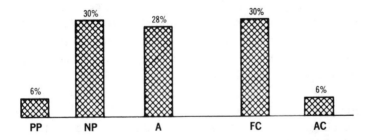

Figure 12. Egogram of the same person, showing change that has occurred during therapy in the percentage of energy in each ego state. PP and AC are now low and NP and FC are both high. A has been released from the directives of the PP and the contamination from the AC and is now more active and effective.

It may seem to you at first sight that this is a difficult thing to do, but actually it is not. After learning about ego states my patients draw their own egograms without hesitation and, as a matter of fact, with considerable gusto. They seem to have an inborn capacity to contact whatever ego states they are in and to be able to express this, once they have adequate information.

When patients show their egograms to other members of the group and ask whether these members experience them as indicated in their egograms, the reply is almost always "Yes."

After you draw your egogram, check it with someone who knows you well and find out if he or she sees you the way you depict yourself.

Now work out your personality formula. Do you like the the percentage of energy you have shown in your various ego states? If not, there are ways of shifting the energy from Critical to Nurturing Parent, and from Adapted to Free Child—of changing from a Frog to a Prince or Princess.

Before going on to describe what information you will need in order to bring about such energy shifts, I shall point out a correlation between the number of crossed transactions a person is involved in and the percentage of his energy bound in the Adapted Child and Critical Parent. My experience is that when the amount of energy in these ego states is high, then the number of crossed transactions is also proportionately high. Here, then, is a cluster indicative of basic personality characteristics: a high amount of energy in the Adapted Child and in the Critical Parent is correlated with a high percentage of crossed transactions.

In fact, I believe that the types of transactions a person engages in depend upon the character of his ego states, and that highly developed Adapted and Rebellious Child and Prejudicial Parent ego states facilitate crossed transactions.

On the other hand, a highly developed Nurturing Parent, Free Child, and Adult will result in a higher percentage of uncrossed (complementary) transactions and a lower percentage of crossed ones.

Regard yourself from the standpoint of these ego states and transactional clusters and you will have another way of gaining insight into your personality. If your transactions are mostly complementary, if you feel good about yourself and enjoy living, then there is a good balance between your Nurturing Parent, Adult, and Free Child ego states.

If you are involved in many crossed transactions and feel, for example, angry, depressed, rejected, as if the weight of the world is on your shoulders, then there is every reason to think that your Critical Parent and Adapted Child ego states are overdeveloped.

The question now is how to change if this is the case.

Recognition of the facts about yourself in terms of the concepts presented thus far is essential, but more information is needed before really significant change is likely to occur.

What information?

One important thing to know is how you structure your time.

## V. TIME STRUCTURING

Most people are uncomfortable with unstructured time, contrary to their own expectations. For example, take the case of a patient of mine who was a businessman. His principal goal in living was to make a lot of money and retire early. He did, after which he found that he didn't know what to do with himself. He became depressed, irritable, lost his zest for living.

I have in my practice clients who have inherited millions of dollars. They do not have to do anything and can sleep all day if they want to. This doesn't make them happy. Their time is unstructured. They come to me to find out what to do.

Why is it that people feel uneasy with unstructured time? Dr. Berne believes that the answer is related to three basic physiological and psychological drives which underlie the need to structure time. These are: (A) stimulus or sensation hunger, (B) recognition hunger, and (C) structure hunger.[7]

### A. Stimulus or Sensation Hunger

Most people seek out stimulation, and this is true of animals, too. A cat comes to life when it is chasing a mouse—a peak experience for a cat. I come to life when the wind is strong, white caps are on the waves, and the spray stings my face while I am sailing in my sloop, *Allegro.* Especially when I am with some stalwart seaman with whom I can share my excitement, who knows that when I greet the waves with yells of excitement it is for fun, and who yells, too.

I come alive when a patient is in the midst of a moving Gestalt experience in which I am playing a crucial part, when I am leading a marathon and having encounters with sixteen or eighteen participants at critical times in their lives, when I am involved in an animated conversation with a colleague, or listening to Beethoven's Fifth Symphony, especially when sharing this experience with someone I love in moments of intimacy.

I come alive when I feel the warm, soft touch of a woman's lips upon mine, and the feel of her hand in my hair.

Stimulation.

Stimulus hunger is basic and needs to be satisfied. It cries out for it. *It* in Gestalt is always *I. I* cry out for stimulation. I do.

How do you satisfy this need for stimuluation? Learning how to do this is a must for owning your own life.

## B. Recognition Hunger

Recognition hunger is also basic. Food isn't enough. This was shown by the now-famous experiments with baby monkeys by Harry Harlow.[8] These monkeys were given a choice between two types of substitute mothers: mannequins made of wire, which supplied them with milk, or cloth mothers, which gave no milk. The baby monkeys clung to the cloth mothers, which were closer in feeling and appearance to their real mothers. The wire mothers wouldn't do, even though they were the source of food.

The experiments of René Spitz prove the same point. He observed and compared two groups of infants and young children kept in a foundling home. In one group the mothers, who were working, came to see their children in the evening. The other group of children had no mothers.

The children in the group with mothers showed an increasing sense of well-being as they grew older. The children of the other group were retarded. Many became listless and apathetic. Some died. Their recognition hunger was not satisfied, nor was their stimulus hunger.[9]

It is essential to satisfy your needs for recognition if you are going to own your own life.

## C. Structure Hunger

Who needs structure? Rats do, for one. Eric Berne gives an example showing the importance of both structure hunger and stimulus hunger in rats "raised in a state of sensory deprivation"; that is, in complete darkness, or in a constantly lighted white cage with no variation. Later in the lives of these animals, after they had been put in ordinary cages with "normal" rats, it was found that they would go to food in a maze if it was placed on a checkerboard, but would not go to food if it was placed on a simple background. Normally, rats would go to food regardless of the background. This showed that the hunger of the deprived rats for a structured stimulus was more important than their hunger for food. The experimenters concluded that the need for structured stimuli (or, as they put it, for "perceptual experience") may involve biological processes just as basic as food hunger. [10]

Berne suggests that time may be structured in six ways: Withdrawal, Rituals, Activities, Pastimes, Games, and Intimacy. Let's examine these in some detail.

### 1. WITHDRAWAL

Withdrawal may be positive or negative in its effects upon the personality. I find it necessary for my own satisfaction in living to withdraw recurrently in order to get in touch with myself, to listen to what my body is telling me, to rearrange and regroup my associations and thoughts, a process I find essential to creative living.

I include under the term "withdrawal," the active process of being alone, surrounded by silence. Then the pine trees swaying in the breeze talk to me, and the movements of the white birch outside of my window, the long, white, slender branches and the dividing twigs of the birch bending in the wind, rebounding in a graceful movement, going beyond the center and coming back again to a balanced quietness, speak to me of the resilience and the unhurried strength of nature. A sea gull flies behind the lacery of the birch tree, sliding gracefully through the air, and in the distance I hear the cawing of crows.

I respond to these movements and sounds of nature. I feel alive. I feel centered, bending and swaying and coming back to equilibrium, like the boughs of the birch. I gather strength.

Then the words of a poem come to me—

> I love you as I love the air I breathe
> Or the sweet sunshine of a daffodil.

I do things in the quietness of being alone that I cannot do as well under any other circumstances. I emphasize especially the opportunity that withdrawal offers for getting in touch with yourself. Withdrawal, in this sense, can be a very valuable use of time.

However, there are reasons for withdrawal that produce, or at least seem to produce, negative effects. I am talking about withdrawing from other people for reasons of fear.

An example of this occurred in a marathon Corlis and I once conducted. During one of the intervals between working, when the members of the group were talking to each other, sharing experiences, I noticed that one of the participants, George, was sitting alone in my study. I talked with him about it. He said, "I feel awkward in a group . . . I don't know what to say. I get embarrassed. I would rather be alone." It is true that he doesn't know what to say and that he feels embarrassed. He spends most of his time home alone, in a rented room. This seems to him the safest thing to do. But is it?

George complains of being isolated. He says that he wants the love of a woman, but he doesn't do anything to get it. He thinks of suicide. Is *that* safe?

What happened to George is that his father had criticized everything he wanted to do and practically everything he said. In consequence, George's Little Professor concluded early in his life that it's safer to keep quiet and to be alone— a "rational" decision under the circumstances. This was true to a large extent when George was a child, subject to his father's irrational rages. But it doesn't hold true any longer. George is now an adult, grown-up person. He has the needs of an adult, grown-up person. They cannot be satisfied in continual isolation.

The answer is not so simple as saying, "Go out into the world, mix with people, find a woman, enjoy life." When George tries to do this he says the wrong things, he makes hurtful remarks, he gets angry irrationally. This comes out of his fear of being rejected, which occurs because he brings it about himself. He needs to learn how to get positive instead of negative strokes. In therapy he is undergoing corrective emotional experiences. For this he needs time and courage, and it is not easy. But this type of withdrawal is not the answer for him.

Withdrawal, as a way of structuring time, then, may be used either constructively or destructively. It may be used as a way of getting in touch with oneself, which is a prerequisite to intimacy with others, or it may be used as a way of avoiding intimacy.

## 2. RITUALS

Rituals are stylized and stereotyped forms of behavior. They are a way of making contact and yet maintaining distance. Probably they are the easiest way of getting and giving strokes. Take, for example, the eight-stroke greeting ritual, so common in the United States and—in one way or another—throughout the world.

John sees an acquaintance coming down the street. When they meet, John says, "Hi, Jim, how are you?" (two strokes). Jim replies, "Hi, John. Fine. How are you?" (two strokes back). Jim: "How's Elizabeth?" (third stroke). John: "Fine. How's Nancy?" (third stroke back). Jim: "Wish I could talk longer. Got to be going. Have a good day" (fourth stroke). John: "You too, Jim" (fourth stroke back—eight strokes altogether). John and Jim made a contact, and they exchanged strokes, but they certainly didn't get close.

Many rituals are used in churches, clubs, and in families. Because everyone is involved with these common symbols and expressions, they foster feelings of belonging and of fellowship.

Family rituals, such as those held at Christmas, Yom Kippur, and Thanksgiving, may foster feelings of closeness, or they may not, depending upon whether people respond from the Free or the Adapted Child, the Critical or the Nurturing Parent. Rituals are simply a habitual way of relating. They can be used to convey personal meaning and feelings, or they can be used to cover up lack of relatedness, or as a façade to cover up a "Not OK" feeling.

Rituals by themselves do not produce closeness, but they can serve as channels toward intimacy if the people involved are capable of intimacy.

Corlis tells me that every fall, as Thanksgiving draws near, she finds herself remembering how Thanksgiving was celebrated in her Sunday school in Louisville, Kentucky. This was before she was five years old. "I can hear the exact sound of all the voices singing," she said.

> Come ye thankful people, come
> Raise the song of harvest home
> All is safely gathered in
> Ere the winter storms begin
> God our Father doth provide
> For our wants to be supplied
> Come ye thankful people, come
> Raise the song of harvest home.

"To this day the sound of the singing brings me a feeling of warmth and being taken care of." A ritual? Yes, but for Corlis a ritual full of personal meaning.

### 3. ACTIVITIES

As a way of structuring time, activities, like withdrawal, can be used destructively or constructively. Here's a good example of how the improper use of an activity can disintegrate a relationship. This occurred in the case of a patient of mine—Don, a twenty-year-old college student. When Don was a boy, his father used to ask him to help repair the family car. Don and his father would be working together, a situation pregnant with the possibility for closeness. Here's what actually happened:

FATHER *(handing* DON *a monkey wrench):* Tighten that nut.

DON: All right. (DON *beginning to tighten the nut.)*

FATHER: You don't know how to do that. Give me the wrench. I'll tighten it myself.

Don is left feeling helpless and angry.

The same activity could be used to bring about closeness as follows:

FATHER *(handing* DON *a monkey wrench):* Will you tighten that nut for me, Don?

DON: All right. (DON *begins to tighten the nut, but has some difficulty with it.)*

(FATHER *sits quietly relaxed while* DON *works out the problem of tightening the nut himself.)*

DON *(completing the task):* That was a tough one.

FATHER: You worked it out, son. I knew you would.

An activity is a set of procedures used to accomplish a given task. The task might be learning a skill, such as playing the violin, or anything from writing an ad to digging in some archeological ruins. Golf, tennis, swimming, sailing, driving a car, playing bridge—these are all activities. Most of the activities we engage in are centered around our work. These activities do not in and of themselves foster intimacy, but those which involve other people offer the opportunity for it.

## 4. Pastimes

Pastimes are conversational ways of passing the time with each other. As a means of structuring time, we can use them to avoid intimacy; or to relate to each other pleasantly in a social situation but without deep involvement; or to discover what the people we are passing the time with really are interested in, in the hope of finding mutual concerns and the exciting possibility of a deeper relationship.

I hardly need go into a long description of pastimes, because they are so familiar to all of us. We play them anywhere and everywhere that two or more people are gathered together—at cocktail parties, dinner parties, in supermarkets, over the back fence, in jet planes, at summer resorts, in senior citizen communities, in offices, in clubs, at home, and abroad.

Eric Berne has identified and given self-explanatory names to many pastimes: Wardrobe, Kitchen, PTA, Ain't It Awful, etc.[11]

In the midst of all our pastimes, sometimes we come upon a stranger whom we feel might become a friend. We listen for clues. A mutual chord is struck. We like his or her looks, style, way of being. We explore further, finding similar hobbies, interests, values . . . or perhaps we find a viewpoint that is intriguingly different and provocative. At any rate there is a feeling of rapport, a hunch that here, in this stranger, lies the possibility of sharing oneself. We want to see this stranger again. And so, while pastiming, a door is opened through which we may venture in search of a deeper experience. This may lead to the rarest and most beautiful of relationships—intimacy.

## 5. GAMES

Games are based upon ulterior transactions, which contain a secret, hidden message intended to influence the other person in some way that he or she doesn't know about. Ulterior transactions are crooked transactions, and since games consist of a series of ulterior transactions that lead to a specific and usually unpleasant outcome—the "payoff"— games are crooked, too.

In a game, the agent pretends to be doing one thing while really doing something else, so that, as Berne says, all games contain a "con." A con only works if there is a receptivity to it in the respondent. This receptivity is called a "gimmick." Such a gimmick may be fear, greed, sentimentality, irritability, interest, involvement, or something else. Once the Agent, or player, hooks the "mark," or Respondent, he pulls some sort of switch, as a result of which he collects his payoff. Following the switch is a moment of confusion, or "crossup," during which the mark tries to figure out what happened to him. Both players then collect their payoffs, and the game ends.[12]

The payoff consists of feelings. In some instances the Initiator collects bad feelings. In other instances he collects (false) good feelings, from having put down the Respondent. In most instances the Respondent collects a bad feeling payoff, as in Why Not, Yes But, where the Agent keeps asking for suggestions and then turning them down, till everyone gets bored or irritated, or Schlemiel, where the Agent soils or damages the Respondent's property or person.

A game can be represented by the following formula:

C plus G = R→S→X→P (Eric Berne's Formula G). "C plus G means that the con hooks into a gimmick, so that the Respondent responds (R). The player then pulls the switch (S), and that is followed by a moment of confusion or crossup (X), after which both players collect their payoffs (P)."

This is illustrated by the following game, called Slug Him, or Whammy. A high school student (the Initiator) says to his teacher (the Respondent), "Do you think I can pass this course?" The teacher replies, "Certainly, if you study hard." The student then says, "What makes you think you know everything?"

The original question is the con. The teacher's interest in the student and his need to be helpful is the gimmick. The teacher's reply is the response. Then the student pulls the switch by saying, "What makes you think you know everything?" (which is also a discount of the teacher's knowledge and capability). The switch causes the teacher to be surprised and confused momentarily, which is the crossup. This is followed by bad feelings on the part of the teacher—the payoff for the teacher—and feelings of elation on the part of the student for having successfully conned the teacher—the payoff for the student.

In terms of ego state transactions, the preceding game would be diagramed as shown in Figure 13, below.

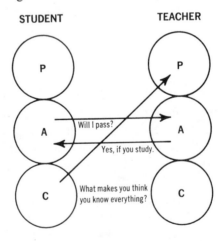

Figure 13. "Slug Him" or "Whammy"

As shown in this figure, the student's original question, "Will I pass?" was an apparently Adult-to-Adult transaction. His real interest (ulterior intention) is to put the teacher down, which he does by the message from his Rebellious Child ego state to her Parent.

In understanding games, it is useful to recognize that they are played from one of three positions: "victim," "rescuer," or "persecutor." During the process of the game these positions shift, so that the victim may become a persecutor, and the rescuer a victim.

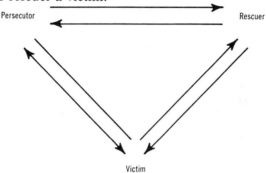

Figure 14. Karpman Drama Triangle

For example, in the case of the game Slug Him just described, the student starts out as a victim and the teacher a rescuer. Then the student switches to a persecutor, and the teacher becomes a victim.

These roles, or positions, can be arranged on a triangle, called the Drama Triangle by Stephen Karpman.[14]

As the game proceeds, the players move around the triangle, switching roles. In the following game, played by an alcoholic and his wife, the alcoholic husband starts out as a victim. His wife says to him, "You always embarrass me at parties by drinking so much." She is the persecutor. Her husband says, "You are right, darling. I won't do that anymore." This is his con, and the start of the game. His wife replies, "I am glad, dear, that you are really listening to me this time." Her gimmick is her interest in him. They go to a party. He drinks excessively. She whispers discreetly into his ear, "You promised me you wouldn't drink so much." He feels she is playing the role of persecutor. He replies, "Stop bugging me. If it weren't for you, I could have some fun around here." This is his switch, since he previously agreed to stop drinking heavily at parties. He is very angry and has shifted into the role of persecutor. His wife has become the victim, and is experiencing a bad feeling payoff in response to her husband's switch and her resultant crossup. She leaves the party upset. The next morning her husband says, "You were right. I shouldn't drink so much." He is the victim again. His wife replies, "It's never too late to change. You'll do better next time." The game starts all over, and the characters go round and round the triangle.

Rapo is a frequently played game. A girl at a party, Sally, flirts with Bill. Her flirtatious manner is her con. Bill responds by going over and talking to her. His gimmick is his interest in her. She invites him to her apartment for a drink after the party. He accepts, and while they are dancing he makes advances to her. She becomes outraged (this is her switch) and orders him out of her apartment at once. Bill experiences a period of confusion (crossup) and leaves her apartment with a bad feeling payoff. Sally, on the other hand, feels indignant, self-righteous, and elated (her payoff). She received an injunction from her mother to not be close to men because "they only think of one thing." Her self-righteous feelings of indignation stem from this, as do her feelings of elation at putting Bill down.

Games can be played to different degrees, called soft or hard. If Sally's flirtation had stopped at the party, this would be the softest (first-degree) version of this game. What really happened as described above is a second-degree version of the game. It is harder than the first, but nothing really serious happened.

If Sally had invited Bill to her apartment knowing that her husband, who has a bad temper and a gun collection, would probably arrive home while they were there together, this would be a third-degree (hard) version of the game and could easily result in Bill's death. The victim of a third-degree Rapo game frequently ends up in the morgue.

Some of the most common games are Kick Me, Now I've Got You, You Son of a Bitch, If It Weren't for You, Why Not, Yes But, Rapo, Court Room, Corner, Blemish, Schlemiel, and Stupid. There are many more games, and if you want to learn what they are and how they are played, read Eric Berne's *Games People Play*.[15]

Since the payoff of games is mostly bad feelings, why, then, do people play them?

There are several reasons:

1. The biological reason for playing games is to get strokes. It is true that many of the strokes are negative, but negative strokes are better than no strokes.

2. The social reason for playing games is time structuring.

3. The existential reason for playing games is to validate the existential position of each player.

Other reasons are:

4. To maintain the rackets (unpleasant feelings inappropriately continued from childhood. See p.106). The payoff of games forwards the rackets.

5. To maintain the first act, the early scenes of childhood.

6. To make people predictable, and thus controllable or unthreatening.

7. To avoid intimacy.

## 6. INTIMACY

Intimacy. What is it? A closeness with someone who matters that pervades the body and the spirit, and which adds to life a quality of existence not to be secured from any other form of being. It is made possible by a sense of empathy and facilitated by a feeling of respect for the other's essential value. It is dependent for its existence upon the presence of another person who has the capacity to give and to receive intimately.

Intimacy means different things to different people. To

me it is based upon authenticity, empathy, and trust. I find
in my practice that patients frequently do not know what
being intimate with another person is really like. They tell
me that although they want to be close, they do not know
how to go about it. Having never observed or experienced
intimacy with their parents as children, they lack a model
and have no clues as to what intimacy is really like.

This is what a special kind of intimacy means to me:

Intimacy is when I can talk to you
And expect what I say to be listened to and understood,
And when you can talk to me and expect what you say
To be listened to and understood.

Intimacy is when I am deeply thrilled with
A sunset or a sunrise and know that
You are deeply thrilled in the same way.

Intimacy is when I can touch you wherever I want to
And know that it will be all right,
And when you can touch me wherever you want to
And know that it will be all right.

Intimacy is when we are having sex
And you are with me in everything I do and feel
And I am with you in everything you do and feel.

Intimacy is when we are having sexual intercourse
And there is a precious conversation between our genitals.

Intimacy is when I caress you and you caress me
And we feel the same deeply personal way about it.

Intimacy is when I write a poem to you and read it to you,
And you listen with deep feelings similar to mine.

Intimacy is when we look at the embers of a fire together
And are close.
Intimacy is when we walk through the fields
Holding hands.

Intimacy is when we read a book together that we both
    like
And discuss it with each other.

Intimacy is when I am at a party with you
And I look across the room

And catch your eye
And we smile at each other.

Intimacy is a shared feeling of coming together
After being apart.

Intimacy is the opposite of "Don't exist." It is existence
at the highest level. It is the opposite of "Don't be you." It
is "Being you" without reservation. It is the opposite of
"Don't show your feelings." It depends upon the freedom
to show feelings. It is the opposite of "Don't belong." The
closeness of intimacy is the essence of belonging.

It is impossible for the Adapted Child to experience
intimacy, for intimacy requires personal integrity and
authenticity. The Adapted Child can experience dependency, not intimacy.

It is impossible for the Rebellious Child to experience
intimacy, for intimacy requires the sharing of feelings of
closeness; rebelliousness is antithetical to sharing.

It is impossible to be intimate and to be in the Critical,
or Prejudicial, Parent. Intimacy depends upon the freedom to be oneself with another person. If you try to
control another person he or she cannot be intimate with
you. The very essence of intimacy is to "be what I am" in
the presence of "what you are." It will not be directed or
controlled.

The capacity for intimacy resides in the Free Child,
which is open and spontaneous, and in the Nurturing
Parent, which is caring and loving. The Adult is important
in helping the person to recognize the circumstances under
which intimacy is appropriate.

Games, with their discounts and put downs, their ulterior transactions and secret messages and devious intentions to use another person, destroy intimacy. Intimacy is "a game-free relationship." [16]

Rackets destroy intimacy. They organize existence around old, currently inappropriate feelings, such as anger, depression, confusion or anxiety, all of which disintegrate the capacity to be intimate.

One cannot be intimate while collecting Brown Stamps (grudges). Intimacy bears no grudges.

Intimacy need not be a rare quality. Every child is born with the capacity for intimacy. Among the most intimate experiences are those between a loving mother and her nursing infant. Children in kindergarten and the first grade are intimate with each other and the teacher. They are open, direct, and spontaneous. If they want to know anything about you, they ask. If they want to tell you anything about themselves, they do it.

Children begin to lose their capacity for intimacy in the second grade, and by the third grade this process is well under way. Ask a third-grader a question. The chances are you will see him computing the answer in his head. He is trying, in his Little Professor, to find out what you want, and play it back to you.

The fact is that as we grow older, we learn not to show our real feelings.

A mother might say to her little girl, who is meeting Aunt Laura for the first time, "Harriet, go and kiss Aunt Laura, and tell her you love her." The child says honestly and directly, "I don't love Aunt Laura. I don't want to kiss her."

Mother, embarrassed, coaxes Harriet. "Of course you do! What a naughty thing to say. Go on now and kiss her. Be a good girl."

Harriet learns early that to win approval from the grownups she must say and do "nice" things she doesn't really feel. This begins the destruction of intimacy.

Feelings of love and affection cannot be forced or directed. In this instance the mother tries to force intimacy when it doesn't exist. What happens is that she teaches the child not to show her real feelings. Having learned not to show real feelings, the child, after growing up, finds it difficult to be intimate.

Introverts are not born, they are made. It takes a lot of effort to repress what one actually feels, but it is clear that spontaneity is extinguished when it is punished or ignored.

And so is intimacy. I personally learned how not to be intimate from my father, who paid little or no attention to what interested me and what I wanted to share with him.

I learned how not to share and not to be intimate. This implies that there was a time when I did share and was intimate. I remember this as a very young child, when I felt very close to Mama, who was warm and loving. I remember losing this capacity for intimacy as I grew up.

Intimacy need not be a rare commodity. I had it, I lost it, I learned it again. So can you, if you want to.

Intimacy is my highest priority. It is, above all other things, what makes life most worthwhile for me.

## VI. SCRIPTS

According to Eric Berne, "the script is a life plan based on a decision made in childhood, re-enforced by the parents, justified by subsequent events, and culminating in a chosen alternative." [17]

Early in life children develop a plan for survival. This is based upon the way they are treated by their parents (that is, how they were stroked). It determines how they will live their lives, whether they will be outgoing or withdrawn, happy or sad, successful or unsuccessful. If children receive an adequate proportion of positive unconditional and positive conditional strokes, their scripts will, in all likelihood, be winners' scripts (*can* scripts). If they receive mostly negative unconditional and negative conditional strokes, their scripts will be losers' scripts (*can't* scripts).

The basic assumption underlying the above statements is that a child with normal psychological and physical capacities will be either a "winner" or a "loser" according to his/her early treatment and early decision.

My experience is that *most persons with a loser's script can change this to a winner's script during the process of therapy.* The manner in which this can be done and the steps involved are now clear, and they will be explained and illustrated in later chapters.

### A. Injunctions

From the standpoint of a person's life plan, a particularly important kind of negative stroke, which may lead to the development of a loser's script, is called the "injunction," or "stopper." [Such injunctions, or prohibitions, go from the Child ego state of the parent (the irrational Child) to the Parent ego state of the child (the electrode) as shown in Figure 15 (Script Matrix).[18]]

Some of the most important injunctions are:

1. Don't exist (don't be).
2. Don't be you.
3. Don't be a child.
4. Don't grow up.
5. Don't trust.
6. Don't make it.
7. Don't think.
8. Don't be important.
9. Don't show your feelings.
10. Don't have your feelings.
11. Don't be sane.
12. Don't enjoy.
13. Just plain don't.[19]

These injunctions are not, for the most part, given by parents to children in the exact words listed above. They are transmitted indirectly, either nonverbally or verbally, usually outside of the parents' awareness. Here are some examples of how these injunctions are given, and typical responses to them:

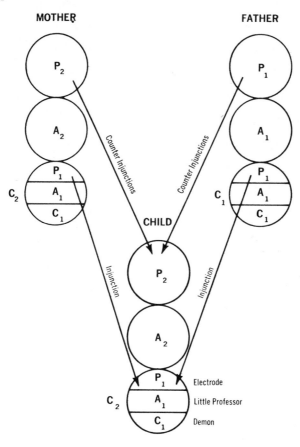

Figure 15. Script Matrix ($P_2$, $A_2$, and $C_2$ refer to the three ego states in the complete person. $P_1$, $A_1$, and $C_1$ refer to the Parent, Adult, and Child in the Child ego state of the whole person)

INJUNCTION #1: Don't exist (don't be).

MANNER IN WHICH GIVEN: The parent says things like, "If it weren't for you, we could have put a new roof on the house last year. See how it is leaking now." "If it weren't for you, we would have more money in the bank." "If it weren't for you, we could have taken a trip around the world." "If it weren't for you, I wouldn't be married to your father." "If it weren't for you, I could be an actress." As you can see, the words, "Don't exist" aren't used but the message is clear.

TYPICAL RESPONSES: [20]

1. "I'll show you if it kills me." As you will remember, I made such a response by working and working and trying to be so outstanding that my father would notice me. Another example is the business executive who is told by his doctor that he should be operated on immediately for an ulcer. He refuses to go until after the board meeting. The ulcer perforates and he dies. His response to an early parental injunction, "I'll show you if it kills me," became part of his script—and it did. By working so hard he was trying to make his father or some other key figure notice him and praise him, and thus change the original injunction "Don't exist" to "Do exist."

2. "If things get too bad, I'll kill myself." This may be the child's response if things are very bad. It is a way out if they become intolerable. It is a kind of safety valve, but may end up in death. Sometimes the child even verbalizes this in a fit of anger or in desperation by saying, "I'll kill myself."

3. "I'll get you even if it kills me." Such a response was verbalized to me by an adolescent boy whose father was a major in the army, very dictatorial and ruthless. This boy said, "I'll get the bastard even if it kills me."

4. "I'll get you to kill me." A wife who had been an unwanted child harried her husband to the point where he screamed at her, "Get out of here or I'll kill you." This is the way this woman expressed in the present her original

response, "I'll get you to kill me," to her parents' "Don't exist" injunction.

5. "If you won't change, I'll kill myself." A patient whose father ignored his accomplishments and who refused to allow him to have any fun as a child and adolescent recently said to me, "Doc, if I can't move out of the room I live in and get myself a girl, I'm going to kill myself." His real message was, "If you won't change, Father, and give me permission to do these things, I'll kill myself." Since his father is dead, the real trouble lies now with his own Prejudicial Parent ego state, which refuses to allow his Child to play.

INJUNCTION #2: "Don't be you."

MANNER IN WHICH GIVEN: The parent says things like, "Be what *I* want you to be." (Be my fantasy.) The mother who wanted a girl and got a boy treats him like a girl and says things like, "Don't play baseball, you might get hurt. Come home right after school and keep me company. Don't ever fight, no matter what anyone does to you. It's bad to fight."

TYPICAL RESPONSE: The child tries to become what the parent wants. If the mother had a boy but wanted a girl, the boy may become effeminate in behavior, may even try to change his sex, or he may become homosexual.

INJUNCTION #3: "Don't be a child."

MANNER IN WHICH GIVEN: Mother says things like, "Now that Daddy is dead, you must be mother's little man." Or father says things like, "As soon as school is out, come and work in the store. Life is for work, not fun."

TYPICAL RESPONSE: Always trying to be grown up and live up to the parents' expectations.

INJUNCTION #4: "Don't grow up."

MANNER IN WHICH GIVEN: Mother, for example, says, "Let me bake the cake for you, you always mess up the kitchen. Anyway, I can do it better, and then you can enjoy eating it more."

TYPICAL RESPONSE: To remain immature, such as avoiding taking responsibility.

INJUNCTION #5: "Don't trust."

MANNER IN WHICH GIVEN: Parents say, for example, "You can't trust men; they're only out for one thing." "You can't trust anyone these days."

TYPICAL RESPONSE: Little girl grows up not trusting men. Child grows up not trusting anyone.

INJUNCTION #6: "Don't make it."

MANNER IN WHICH GIVEN: Mother or father or both say things like, "It's too bad you aren't as smart as your brother. You'll never be able to get good grades."

TYPICAL RESPONSE: To sabotage whatever is happening that's good, and thus "manage" not to make it.

INJUNCTION #7: "Don't think."

MANNER IN WHICH GIVEN: Parent says things like, "Let me do your homework for you, darling. It's too hard for you."

TYPICAL RESPONSE: To act without thinking. To avoid thinking.

INJUNCTION #8: "Don't be important."

MANNER IN WHICH GIVEN: Parents say things like, "Children should be seen and not heard." This is given by parents who are concerned with their own importance and don't pay attention to their children.

TYPICAL RESPONSE: Person doesn't recognize his own importance. Plays himself down.

INJUNCTION #9: "Don't show your feelings."

MANNER IN WHICH GIVEN: This is often given without verbalizing by parents who don't show their own feelings.

Or a mother might say to her child, "Don't show your feelings or it will kill your father."

TYPICAL RESPONSE: Child feels it is wrong to show feelings and blocks his feelings.

INJUNCTION #10: "Don't have your feelings." (This is worse than "Don't show your feelings.")

MANNER IN WHICH GIVEN: Given by example by parents who don't feel their feelings themselves, and by parents who punish their children severely for showing any feelings. Also by parents who say to their children who fall and hurt themselves, "It doesn't really hurt."

TYPICAL RESPONSE: Child doesn't know what feelings are.

INJUNCTION #11: "Don't be sane."

MANNER IN WHICH GIVEN: Mother may say, "Your father's side of the family has a lot of crazy people in it. Your father's crazy, too. You're just like your father."

TYPICAL RESPONSE: To go crazy. I am reminded of a patient of mine, a girl whose father kept telling her that she was ugly and unattractive, that men would never like her, that she was crazy. She became crazy.

INJUNCTION #12: "Don't enjoy."

MANNER IN WHICH GIVEN: This message is often given by parents who believe that life is hard and full of suffering and disappointment. They express the message by example and word that life is to be endured and not enjoyed.

TYPICAL RESPONSE: "I don't dare enjoy myself because if I do I'll be disappointed. That's the way life is."

INJUNCTION #13: "Just plain don't."

MANNER IN WHICH GIVEN: Parent says things like, "Go find Tom and tell him to stop whatever he's doing."

TYPICAL RESPONSE: Fear of doing things.

These early injunctions are of crucial importance in determining the life script. When a child receives one or more injunctions, the usual response is to follow them throughout life as a way of survival, as a way of receiving strokes. Although other strokes are sometimes available from other persons, the strokes from parents or guardians are the ones that are most effective, because these are the ones the young child needs for survival. They are the key adults in his/her world; they tell the child who he/she is.

Occasionally, a child may decide not to follow his parent's injunctions. In such a case he may absent himself from his home during a large part of the time and go up the street and listen to the parents of a friend, who give him different messages. Or he may just say to himself that Mother is in one of her crazy spells again and not buy the injunctions. If he does accept them, the power of the injunctions is so strong that even after he is grown and has other options for survival, he still directs his life according to them.

On the basis of the injunctions a child receives, and his Early Decision about them, he works out his life plan, or life script.

## B. Life Scripts— Winners, Non-winners, and Losers

It may be surprising to you to know that a child develops the plan for his life and how he will live it when he is still very young. But this is exactly what happens. The basic material from which the child molds his life plan is the way he is treated by his parents. The nature of the plan will depend to a large extent upon what injunctions he received, and what kind of strokes his parents (and other important people in his life) gave him.

If he received a "Don't exist" injunction, it will be one plan; if he received a "Don't be you" injunction, it will be another plan. And if he received several injunctions, as of course most children do, his life plan will reflect the combined effects of each injunction.

The basic principle is that the life plan in general will include a way of following out the injunction, whether it is just one, or—as is usually the case—more than one.

According to Berne,[21] a person may have a winner's script, a non-winner's script, or a loser's script. Winners know what they want, go after it, and get it. Losers may go after what they want, but somehow they fail to achieve it. Non-winners settle for a banal script. They neither win nor lose.

Being a winner is not based upon the concept of winning against others in a competitive sense. It has to do with achieving personal goals and fulfilling one's personal potential. A winner is autonomous, authentic, aware, responsive to life, and capable of intimacy.

Berne describes five loser scripts and a non-winner script. These are the Never, the Always, the Until, the After, the Over and Over, and the Open End scripts.

People who have Never scripts are never able to get for themselves the things they want the most because they have been forbidden by their parents to do this. The Child in them is *afraid* of what they want most because of parental injunctions against securing them.

People who have Always scripts have usually had spiteful parents who, when threatened, said such things as, "If that's what you insist on doing, go ahead and do it the rest of your life."

People who have Until scripts have parents who told them that they could not have what they want until they have done something else first, such as, "You can't get married until you have finished college," or, "You can't have sex until you are married," or, "You can't leave home before your grandmother dies, because we need you here to help us take care of her," or "You can't get married before your father dies."

People with After scripts have parents who insisted that "If you enjoy yourself, then after that your troubles will begin."

People with Over and Over scripts have parents who

scripted them to "Never quite make it." And so they try over and over again.

The non-winner has an Open End script. Having carried out parental instructions to old age, he doesn't know what to do next while waiting for his "final just reward." Mothers whose children have grown up and left home and who don't know what to do with themselves are in this category. So are business people who have obediently put in their thirty years with the company, have retired, and then literally don't know what to with themselves.

Each of these six scripts has its sexual aspects, which Berne noted and described.

"Never scripts may forbid either love or sex, or both. If they forbid love but not sex, they are a license for promiscuity, a license which some sailors and soldiers and wanderers take full advantage of, and which prostitutes and courtesans use to make a living. If they forbid sex but not love, they produce priests, monks, nuns, and people who do good deeds such as raising orphan children.

"Always scripts are typified by young people who are driven out of their homes for the sins which their parents have prompted them to commit. 'If you're pregnant and not married, go earn your living on the streets.' ('The father who turns his daughter into the storm may have had lecherous thoughts about her since she was ten. . .')

"The parental sexual programming in Until scripts is the loudest of all, since it usually consists of outright commands: 'You can't have sex until you're married, and you can't get married as long as you have to take care of your mother (or until you finish college).'

"The parental influence in After scripts is almost as outspoken . . . 'After you get married and have children, your troubles will begin.'

"Over and Over scripts produce always a bridesmaid and never a bride, and others who try hard again and again, and never quite make it.

"Open-ended scripts end with aging men and women

who lose their vitality without much regret and are content with reminiscing about past conquests.

"At the more intimate level, each of these scripts has its own bearing on the physical experience of sex—the ability to have orgasms, for example. The Never script makes spinsters and bachelors and prostitutes and pimps, and frigid women who never have an orgasm.

"The Until script favors harried housewives and tired businessmen, neither of whom can get sexually aroused until every last detail of the household or the office has been put in order.

"The sexual potency, drive, and power of a human being are to some extent determined by his inheritance and his chemistry, but they seem even more strongly influenced by the script decisions he makes in early childhood, and by parental programming which brings about such decisions." [21]

## C. Fairy Tales

Once having decided on the nature of his life script, the child frequently looks around for someone to show him or her how to follow it out. Such a model may be a character in a fairy tale, or a favorite character in a book, a television show, a motion picture or a comic strip, or a sports or show business celebrity.

In the case of a girl who received the injunction, "Don't grow up," her favorite fairy tale was "Sleeping Beauty." She waits for the Prince to come along, she waits for magic, but in real life there is no Prince and there is no fairy tale magic.

## D. Counterinjunctions and Counterscripts

Other messages which parents give to children are called counterinjunctions. As the name implies, they are messages which are "counter to the injunctions," that is, they function in the opposite way from the injunctions. Counterinjunctions to the injunction "Don't exist" are "I like you as you are" or "I like to have you around." A counterinjunction to the injunction "Don't be you" is "Of course you must be whatever you want to be. That is the most important thing."

When a parent gives a counterinjunction she knows what she is doing; she (or he) is aware of it.

The counterinjunction goes from the Parent ego state of the parent to the Parent ego state of the child, as shown in Figure 15, p. 93 (Script Matrix).

On the basis of the counterinjunctions, the child develops a counterscript, which is the opposite of the script.

As the child grows up, he will spend part of his time in his script and part in his counterscript. The messages of the injunctions are given with more intensity than the counterinjunctions, since the parent himself (herself) has a strong investment in seeing to it that the child accepts and adapts to them. This investment is the unconscious feeling on the part of the parent that if the child does not accept the injunctions, the parent will feel that there is something wrong with *him* or *her*. Therefore the parent presses harder, unaware of its affect on the child.

Because of this, and because the child is exposed to injunctions earlier than to counterinjunctions (prior to the child's being able to understand words), he will usually slip back into his script.

For example, a girl who is given the injunction "Don't trust men" and the counterinjunction "Get married" will distrust men and do things to offend them and keep them at a distance. Thus, she may invite a man to her apartment and offer him a drink and dance with him. Then when he makes advances to her she gets angry and tells him to leave immediately.

Nevertheless, the counterinjunction still affects her, and she wants to get married. Finally, a man comes along who, for his own reasons—possibly his own masochism—puts up with her castrating behavior and falls in love with her. She marries him and for a short time is happy. She is in her counterscript. But as time goes on she finds more and more (unreal) reasons to distrust him, and the marriage becomes more and more stormy. Finally he divorces her. Her "Don't trust men" script has taken over again.

### E. Miniscripts

A recent contribution to counterscript theory is the mini-script, described by Taibi Kahler and Hedges Capers.[22]

A miniscript is a brief sequence of behavior that occurs in seconds or minutes which re-enforces the life script. It may be an OK miniscript, re-enforcing an OK life plan, or it may be a not-OK miniscript, re-enforcing a not-OK script.

Miniscripts can be easily picked up by listening to what people say. In a recent workshop I asked for volunteers to talk to me for a few minutes in order to pick up their miniscripts. No one volunteered, and so I turned to a person in the audience I considered to be especially well established and secure and said, "Will you talk to me?" He hesitated a moment and then said, "I never say anything first." I laughed, and so did everyone else, for the first words out of his mouth were a miniscript. His miniscript forwarded a life script which contained as an important element the message "Don't be first," probably in re-sponse to an injunction such as, "Don't be better than your father."

Sam, a businessman and a patient of mine, said, "I never enjoy a vacation because on the third day out I start worrying about the office." I would intuit from this miniscript that Sam has "Don't exist," "Don't make it," and "Don't enjoy" injunctions. He also has a "Try hard" counterscript driver.

According to Kahler and Capers there are five coun-terscript drivers, which on first sight might appear to be healthy admonitions but which on closer examination are shown to actually forward the Not-OK life script. These are, "Be perfect, Try hard, Hurry up," "Please me," and "Be strong." They originate in the parent's Parent ego state and are directed to the Parent ego state of the child. The developing person uses these drivers to maintain an "I'm OK" feeling, but there's a catch—the person who receives one or more of these drivers only feels OK *if* he is following them. The existential position is really, "I'm OK—if." That is, the person who receives a "Be perfect" driver only feels OK if he is perfect in whatever he does, which he obviously cannot be. Hence he ends up feeling Not-OK.

This information is summarized in the "Not-OK" Miniscript Formula and the "Miniscript Triangle" (Fig. 16) which shows the four miniscript positions and the corresponding existential positions.

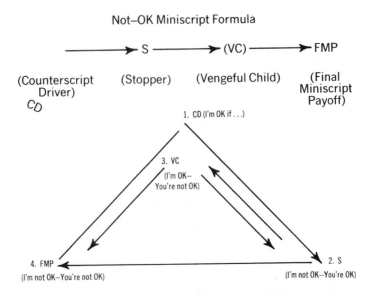

Figure 16. Miniscript Triangle

The case of the businessman, Sam, mentioned above, illustrates the use of the miniscript triangle. His No. 1 position (counterscript driver) in the miniscript triangle is, "I am only OK if I try hard and don't waste time enjoying myself." So when he went on vacation he felt anxious and guilty. He was unable to overcome this feeling and so went into the stopper, or injunction. His injunctions were "Don't exist," "Don't make it," and "Don't enjoy." He doesn't know that he is irritated and anxious because of the effect of these injunctions upon him, since they are out of his awareness. He has to blame his bad feelings on something, so he blames them on the hotel, the weather, and his wife. When he does this, he is in position No. 3, the Vengeful Child. His wife becomes furious and exclaims in anger, "This is the last time I'm going on a vacation with you." Then Sam moves to position No. 4 of the miniscript triangle, the Final Miniscript Payoff, and feels isolated and abandoned.

In position No. 1 Sam's existential position is, "I'm OK if I fulfill the miniscript driver's demands." In position No. 2 his existential position is, "You're OK—I'm Not OK." In position No. 3 it is, "I'm OK—You're Not OK." In position No. 4 it is, "I'm Not OK—You're Not OK."

What can Sam do to resolve his problem? Kahler and Capers say that the person in position No. 1, where he is acting under the influence of his miniscript drivers, can sometimes resolve his problem by giving himself "allowers" (or permissions) which are the opposite of the miniscript drivers. In Sam's case he needed an allower like "It's OK not to try hard and work hard all the time; it's OK to do things without 'Trying hard.'"

In Sam's case, giving this allower didn't resolve his difficulties because he ran smack into his injunctions, "Don't exist," "Don't make it," and "Don't enjoy."

Before Sam will be able to enjoy a vacation without anxiety he must resolve these injunctions and come to a redecision about his life script, so that he won't re-enforce it with his miniscript behavior.

At the time he went on vacation he had not done this, and so he went successively into the second, third, and fourth positions of the miniscript triangle. Subsequently he worked on and resolved his injunctions. He was then in a position to deal with his counterscript driver, "Try hard," and at this time was able to accept the allower (permission) to enjoy himself and be successful by "Doing" rather than "Trying hard."

As children grow up, they forward their life scripts with games, *rackets,* and by collecting *trading stamps.*

## E. Rackets

Rackets are bad feelings which the child developed in response to the way his parents (or other key persons) treated him. They stay with him as he grows up and lead to no constructive action. Some of the most common rackets are persistent feelings of sadness, inadequacy, depression, regret, anxiety, confusion, anger, helplessness, fear, and guilt.

If a person has a depressed racket he will look for something to be depressed about. Thus, if it is raining he might say, "Isn't it too bad it is raining and the flowers aren't getting any sunshine." Or if the sun is out, "Isn't it a shame the flowers aren't getting any water." No matter what the facts are, the person with a depressed racket will find something to be depressed about.

Since rackets persist into adulthood and even old age, they play a very important part in how a person reacts throughout his or her entire life.

Rackets exist outside of the awareness of the person who has them. If a man has a depressed racket, he will not know that he is looking for something to be depressed about; if he has an anger racket, he will not know that he is looking for something to be angry about.

If a person is in a racket, he or she may do strange things and think they are perfectly normal. Thus, a patient of mine who had an anger racket used to walk across the street when the light turned green and angrily hit the car that had stopped closest to him with a folded newspaper.

Rackets can be picked up by determining whether or not the intensity of a person's reaction is exaggerated beyond what is justified by the actual circumstances.

It would be difficult to overestimate the devastating effect that rackets produce in our lives. They actually keep us feeling sad, depressed, anxious, confused, regretful, angry, helpless, afraid, and so on, without any adequate external reason for this.

Why do we perpetuate these bad feelings called rackets? We do it because of the homeostatic tendency in all persons to maintain the existential position established in early childhood.

As I think about patients in my practice who have gotten over their rackets in therapy, I am impressed with the similarity between the way they feel and the way a person feels who has just awakened from a nightmare—a feeling of wonder and relief, as if being released from a spell. It is, in a sense, a release from the witch's curse—the messages and commands from the irrational Child of the parent.

### F. Trading Stamps (Collecting)

Trading stamps are hoarded feelings—usually bad feelings (brown stamps), angry feelings (red stamps) or depressed feelings (blue stamps)—that are saved up with the idea of trading them in later for some psychological reward, such as a "free" temper tantrum—just as people who save up trading stamps from the grocery store trade them in for a free radio or something else they want.

Usually the payoff of a game is bad feelings, and such bad feelings are called stamps. Sometimes the payoff of a game is counterfeit good feelings, such as elation at putting someone else down. These feelings are called "counterfeit gold stamps," in contrast to real gold stamps, good feelings which result from doing something well and being complimented for it.

Just as people who collect trading stamps from stores paste them in books, so people who collect psychological trading stamps may be thought of as pasting them in books, too. One book of brown stamps is worth a free temper tantrum, five books is worth being fired from a job, ten books is worth a free divorce, and fifty books is worth a free suicide.

Trading stamps are closely related to rackets. Thus, they are used to justify discharging pent-up feelings which one has as a result of his racket. A person with an anger racket will cash in a book of stamps for a guilt-free temper outburst. The stamps are just an excuse for discharging the anger he already has.

Games forward the rackets, and stamps are the currency by means of which this is done. Games, stamps, and rackets all act together in a system that many people use to keep themselves feeling bad.

### G. Existential Positions

Eric Berne describes four existential positions: (1) "I'm OK—You're OK," (2) "I'm OK—You're Not OK," (3) "I'm Not OK—You're OK," and (4) "I'm Not OK—You're Not OK." [23]

1. "I'm OK—You're OK." This is the position of health, the position toward which one works in therapy, and which many patients achieve.

What does "I'm OK" mean? It means that I feel all right about myself. It means that I accept myself for what I am. I may not be perfect; in fact, I know I'm not. But I accept my imperfections and do whatever I can about them and stop worrying about them. It means that I am autonomous. It means that I know I have a right to exist. It means that I know I have a right to my own thoughts, feelings, and actions, and that I recognize the same rights in others.

What does "You're OK" mean? It means that it's OK with me for you to lead your own life—that I respect you for what you are, and, hopefully, that we can relate as autonomous equals.

The "I'm OK—You're OK" position is an extremely important one which reflects a positive attitude toward oneself and others, and, in consequence, toward the world in general.

A person in this position has a satisfactorily functioning Nurturing Parent, Adult, and Free Child. For the most part, this person does not play games, have rackets, or collect brown stamps. His or her script will be a winner's script.

The "I'm OK—You're OK" position has much of its origin at mother's breast; it is nourished by the milk of positive unconditional and positive conditional stroking.

2. "I'm OK—You're Not OK." This is the position of the person who feels that everyone else is beneath him, who looks for things to criticize and make fun of in a spouse or others. Such people, Eric Berne says, are meddlers in other people's business. They start crusades against imagined enemies or those whom they feel are inferior. At their worst they are killers.[24]

The person in this position has an overdeveloped Critical Parent. He is certain to have an anger racket, and to be an avid collector of brown stamps.

It was first called to our attention by Heges Capers that many people in the American culture are in this existential position part of the time. For example, certain people look down on Italians, or Jews, or Catholics, or Protestants, or WASPs, or the Establishment, or businessmen or artists, depending, in fact, upon their own degree of Not-OKness. This concept could be formulated: I'm Not OK; therefore You're Not OK, although the person himself is unaware of being in this position.

3. "I'm Not OK—You're OK." By far the largest number of persons who come to my office are in this

position. They feel that what they say somehow doesn't count, and that the other person knows better. They depreciate themselves and find it difficult to accept compliments. This is a self-abasing, depressive position and it is typically neurotic.

Children develop this position as a result of parental injunctions such as 'Don't exist," "Don't be you," "Don't grow up," "Don't show your feelings," "Don't belong."

People in this position play such games as Kick Me, Stupid, and Why Don't You, Yes But. They may have many types of rackets, such as a depressed racket, an anger racket, an inadequacy racket, a confused racket, and so on. They have received too many conditional positive and negative strokes, and not enough positive unconditional ones.

4. "I'm Not OK—You're not OK." This is a position of hopelessness and futility. A person in this position might think, "Why not go crazy, or why not kill myself." It is produced by severe negative conditional and unconditional stroking such as, "If you don't get out of bed, I'll knock your goddamn teeth out" or "You're always in the way—get out of the house and stay out or I'll beat your brains to a pulp."

I once had a patient in this position whose father had tried to throw him into the furnace when he was a child. He didn't succeed because the boy had spread his legs and his father couldn't get him through the furnace door.

This position has all the elements of a loser's script.

Patients in this position play such games as, Look How Hard I Tried, Look What You Made Me Do, and If It Weren't For You. They are full of rackets, which are particularly intense.

The second, third, and fourth existential positions are all subject to improvement in therapy. My experience, however, is that people in the second position do not voluntarily come for therapy. Those in the third and fourth positions usually do.

Whatever the position, those who really wish to change can, with adequate help.

### G. Symbiosis, Discounting, and Passivity

There is a position in which two people feel (often out of awareness) "I'm Not OK Without You—You're Not OK Without Me." This is one essential ingredient of a condition described by Aaron and Jackie Schiff as symbiosis.[25] Symbiosis is a dependency relationship in which one person (initially the child) operates mainly from her/his Child ego state, and the other one (initially the mother) operates mainly from her Parent and Adult. Thus, between the two of them they have functioning Parent, Adult, and Child ego states which together constitute one total personality. The remaining ego states in both people are kept passive; they do not function in any way that would threaten the dependency contract. Such a symbolic relationship is illustrated in Figure 17.

The initial symbiosis was between mother and infant, and this is normal and healthy. It is illustrated by the Nurturing Parent and Adult responding to the infant's cry for milk or for some other form of stroking. Without such a symbiotic relationship the infant would not have survived. However, as the infant grows up *traumatic separation* from the mother or *unresponsiveness* by her to the child's needs may block healthy growth and development by the child and maintain the symbiotic relationship. This is often re-enforced by *neglect* or *overprotection* by the mother, which interferes with the child's recognizing himself as a separate person from his mother. In such a case the symbiosis is maintained into adulthood and the person remains psychologically dependent upon his/her mother (or father) and also tries to develop symbiotic

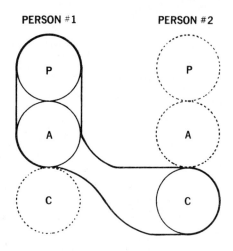

Figure 17. Symbiosis

relationships with others, such as his/her spouse and employer.

When this occurs the person has an investment in maintaining the symbiosis, and is made very anxious by anything that threatens it. The same is true for his/her symbiotic partner.

The Schiffs say that all games develop out of unresolved symbiotic relationships, and that games are an attempt to re-enact the symbiotic relationship in order to be taken care of, or as a way of expressing anger at the existence of interdependency. For example, the game Schlemiel, in which the player soils or destroys his host's property, is an attempt to set up a situation in which he is forgiven (taken care of). The game Why Don't You, Yes But, in which the initiator asks for help and then frustrates the helper by not following any of his suggestions, is a way of expressing anger from Child to Parent. The source of the anger is resentment at the original symbiosis.

The symbiotic relationship is maintained by the *discounting* of the child by the parent figure, initially by the real parent and later by the child's internalized Parent. When one person discounts another he acts as if what *he* feels is more important than what the other person feels, says or does; hence he does not really pay attention to what the other person wants—that is, he "discounts" him. The growing-up child, on his part, maintains the symbiosis by not taking responsibility for his own behavior, that is, by attributing the cause of his feelings and actions to others or to environmental circumstances. The Schiffs call this "grandiosity." The parental position is, "I have to be in control of you in order to feel secure" (an exaggeration), and the child's position is, "Without you I am nothing" (also an exaggeration). This latter position is especially obvious in the adult person who is behaving like a child, as in the case of the employee who is always running to his boss for reassurance that he is doing his job right.

Anything that might interrupt the symbiosis is reacted to with extreme anxiety. The Schiffs say that persons are passive because they are afraid that if they become active and take responsibility for their thoughts and behavior, they will destroy the symbiosis. The thought of this sends them into a panic. Therefore they do nothing (remain passive).

The Schiffs maintain that in the average American population one out of four statements is a discount. The purpose of the discounter is to maintain a symbiosis. If the person who is discounted overexaggerates the importance of the discount (as if he were a child being discounted by his mother), this is pathological. A healthy reaction would be to call the other person's attention to the discount (confront the discount).

The conclusions that flow out of these concepts are very important: (1) a significant cause of emotional disturbances is the unhealthy continuance into adolescence and adulthood of pathological symbiotic relationships; (2) symbioses are maintained by discounting, by grandiosity, and by passive behavior.

Two types of passive behavior identified by the Schiffs are doing nothing and overadaptation. The overadapted person tries to please others instead of himself, works toward achieving goals that he believes will please others rather than himself.

The Schiffs say that the resolution of the passivity in therapy occurs initially through the active intervention of the therapist, that is, that the stimulus for interruption of the passivity must come from the environment. It is a mistake for the therapist to try to out-passive a passive person; on the contrary, he or she should should facilitate awareness by the passive person that what is required of him by the environment is active participation and problem-solving. This is the way the grandiosity is broken down.

The passive person makes other people uncomfortable by refusing to take responsibility. In order to disrupt the symbiosis, the Schiffs say, the passive person must be made to feel more uncomfortable than he makes others. This is done by confronting (exposing) every instance of discounting by the passive person. The passive person is then told to explain logically why he is discounting, which involves taking account of his feelings and the feelings of the other people involved.

The most effective attitude for a therapist to take with a passive person is one of expectation and support.[26]

## H. Contracts

A contract is an agreement between a client and his therapist to work together to bring about the resolution of some specific problem which the client wants to solve, or to help the client change in some way that he or she wants to change. I frequently begin a group marathon by asking each of the members how he or she would like to be different when driving home after the marathon. The formulations of how each person would like to be different and his or her agreement to work with me on ways to bring this about is a contract.

One person might say, "I would like to feel closer to people." Then I might say, "Will you think of ways that you can be closer to people right here in this marathon and follow through on these ways, so that by observing your actions we can see that you are different."

Or, I might ask someone if he would like to start working on this contract right away. If he says, "Yes," then I might say, "Go directly to each person in the group and say, 'I want to be closer to you during this marathon,' and see what response you get back." The usual reaction is that when such a person has gone halfway around the group he feels so much more comfortable that he is already feeling closer, and says so.

By entering into a contract with a patient, who then states specifically what he wants to work on, the TA therapist avoids the pitfall of becoming involved in long, rambling, abstract, and often irrelevant transactions, instead of definite and concrete ones. This procedure accelerates the progress of the therapy.

## I. Permission, Potency, and Protection

The TA therapist does three things that are important facilitators of change in the patient:

1. *He gives him or her permission to change.* Thus, in the case of a person who was given "Don't be close" and "Don't show your feelings" injunctions, he might say, "It's all right to be close and it's all right to show your feelings."

2. *He exhibits his potency,* in this case by showing clearly and openly his conviction that it certainly *is* all right to be close and show feelings. And he illustrates this by his own actions.

3. When the patient becomes anxious upon breaking injunctions and giving up the irrational behavior based upon them, *the therapist protects him* by assuring him that

this is a good thing to do and he need fear no ill consequences if he processes what he does through his Adult.

## J. The Redecision

According to Robert Goulding,[27] one of the most important things a patient does in bringing about change—perhaps the most important thing—is to make a "redecision," which then replaces his "early decision" to adapt himself to his parents' injunctions. This "redecision" must be the patient's "own" redecision, otherwise it will not be effective.

Such a redecision alters the character of the life script and is decisive in the change from a loser's to a winner's script.

In order to be binding, this decision must be approved by the person's Free Child, Adult, and Parent.

The redecision frequently originates in the Free Child during a time of deep emotional experience, such as occurs when a patient is "closing a gestalt" with a parent during Gestalt "double-chair" work. This is dramatically illustrated in the case of George (see Chapter Six) when he is expressing deep feelings toward his father and finally says, "I will no longer allow you to dictate the way I lead my life."

A way of facilitating the patient's making a redecision used by Robert Goulding is to ask him how he will be in five years if he doesn't change; how he will be in ten years if he doesn't change; how he will be in fifteen years if he doesn't change. By this time, the patient is frequently so horror-stricken at the prospect that he makes a redecision.

The redecision involves a deep understanding of the significant elements that have shaped one's life and a willingness to give up those that are detrimental.

This redecision needs to be implemented with specific ways of facilitating it. In my own life, this occurred in the workshop with Bob and Mary Goulding that follows.

# CHAPTER
# 5

# *TA and Gestalt Workshop with Robert and Mary Goulding*

I first met Bob and Mary Goulding at an informal dinner at the New Orleans meeting of the American Group Psychotherapy Association, where I sat across the table from them. I had gone to the meeting to be chairman of the section on films, but by far the most important thing for me was meeting Bob and Mary, though how important I didn't realize at the time.

I told them how I had changed my methods of doing group therapy as a result of my experiences at Esalen. Bob told me what he and Mary were doing. There were some similarities to what I was doing, and some differences, especially with regard to Transactional Analysis, about which I knew very little at the time.

"Come to one of our workshops," Bob suggested. I did, the following spring (1970), the week after the American Psychiatric Association Annual Meeting in San Francisco.

The day after the meeting closed I left for Mt. Madonna, where Bob and Mary had bought a large ranch house for their Western Institute for Group and Family Therapy. In fact, they had just taken possession of it the day I arrived. It is a one-story ranch house, something like a Mexican villa, nestled on the side of Mt. Madonna, overlooking the town of Watsonville, California, and the Pacific Ocean. The house was surrounded by many acres of hilly, green pasture, with a stand of huge eucalyptus trees at one end of the property. Every morning the sun rose behind these trees, its rays penetrating between them with golden shafts, which moved me deeply. The house was encompassed by a lawn upon which stood a huge maple and one tall palm tree—an ever-present sentinel, adding to the place a kind of informal grandeur which was very soothing.

On the periphery of the lawn were several cottages, making it possible for Bob and Mary to accommodate about forty people. At one end of the lawn was a remodeled barn, used for workshops and seminars. As the workshop developed, we met there every night, except Wednesday, for general discussion of TA principles and related subjects.

The land adjacent to the barn looked out over a series of rolling pastures, farms, and hills, which seemed to have been untouched by time. Quiet, peaceful hills, undulating one after another to the Pacific Ocean.

Bob met me at the door with a casual, "Hi, Dick." We hugged each other momentarily. "We just bought this place last week," Bob said. "When our real estate agent told us it was on the market we came up and looked at it and decided to buy it right away. It's lucky we did, because several other people tried to buy it just after we closed the deal." One of Bob's characteristics is his capacity to know what he wants when he sees it and to make a quick decision.

Bob is a large man, over six feet tall, muscular and very active. He once told me an interesting story about an experience he had with Fritz Perls at Esalen when he was acting as his co-therapist in a workshop there. Fritz was characteristically a showman, and liked to be at the center of the stage. As the workshop progressed, Bob noticed that Fritz talked to him less and less, and finally not at all. Bob didn't know what was wrong, but decided he would try to do something about it. He went to Fritz and said that he thought Fritz was the best therapist he knew. Fritz relaxed at once and said he felt the same way about Bob. After that everything was fine. Bob had given Fritz a positive stroke, and Fritz had given Bob a positive stroke back—a very appropriate TA transaction. This illustrates another characteristic of Bob's—a highly developed intuitive sense of knowing where the other person is.

For many years Bob Goulding and Eric Berne were associates in Carmel, California, and Bob has been a very significant figure in the development of TA theory and practice.

Formerly a practicing medical doctor, Bob now devotes himself entirely to teaching Transactional Analysis and associated methods of therapy with his wife, Mary Edwards Goulding, who holds a master's degree in social work and who is a Teaching Member and Vice-President of the International Transactional Analysis Association.

I was assigned a room with three other men, who arrived shortly after I did. John was a minister from Memphis, Tennessee; tall, well-built and outgoing. Charles was from Dallas, Texas; he was a medical doctor who wanted to learn about TA and use it in his practice. Dave, from New Orleans, was a clinical psychologist.

At nine the next morning twenty-eight of us assembled in the thirty-five-foot-long living room with a large picture window at one end. When we looked through the window on a clear day we could see the Pacific Ocean in the distance.

My primary interest in TA, at this point, was as a therapy technique which I would use with my own patients. I had no idea how deeply it would affect me, and how much it would change my life.

Bob and Mary began the seminar by describing the ego states, with which you are already familiar. I wondered what parental slogans I had gotten from my father. One of the most important was "Try hard." "If you try hard, everything will turn out right," Papa would say. "You aren't going to college to join a fraternity. You are going there to learn."

What messages did I get from my mother's Parent? "Be a nice boy, be sweet, be good." "Don't complain." "Suffer in silence. It's better to be a martyr than to do something about what bothers you."

When Bob talked about the Adult ego state, I had no trouble understanding that at all. I was brought up on the importance of staying in my Adult. Most of my transactions had been carried out in my Adult—too many to make life really interesting.

"The Child ego state," Bob said, "is what constitutes the intrinsic *me.*" Well, I thought, that's what I am looking for.

"What comes from the outside constitutes the Parent," Bob continued. This narrows down my problem, I thought. What I have had is too much Parent and Adult, and too little of the spontaneous, playful Child. I had begun to discover my spontaneous Child at Esalen, but it was still largely repressed.

As you will remember, injunctions are secret messages that originate in the irrational Child ego state of the parent and are delivered to the Child ego state of the child; they become fixated in the electrode (the Parent of the Child of the child). A diagram illustrating these terms is given on page 93 . The parent is usually unaware that he or she is giving such messages to the child, though occasionally he or she actually verbalizes them.

Bob next began to talk about the injunctions. As he did, I thought about which ones applied to me.

The first injunction Bob described was, "Don't exist," or "Don't be." This is the one most frequently given.

"Sometimes the child gets 'Don't exist' messages from both parents," Bob said. "The effect of this double message is extremely powerful and the child may feel that he can't exist. In the absence of therapeutic (or some other fortuitous intervention) he will probably kill himself in some way or another later in life, like the man who drives his car at high speed on the wrong side of the road and is killed in a smashup.

"One response to the 'Don't exist' injunction," Bob continued, "is, 'I'll show you if it kills me.'"

"Kids often get a 'Don't exist' message from one parent, and a 'Do exist' message from the other. Then the child has to make a choice, and that choice is very important and it may be made very early."

As I sat listening, I recorded this without any particular feeling, one way or another. It was only after I thought about it later, as I was walking to my cabin, that I began to wonder whether I had gotten a "Don't exist" injunction from my father.

That night, as I sat on my bed, a memory suddenly came back to me. I remembered teasing my father to buy me a bicycle when I was six. He can easily get one for me, I thought, all I have to do is to get him to say yes. I didn't know then how hard pressed he was for money. I thought he could do anything he wanted. I kept pressing. Suddenly he looked at me angrily and said, "If you keep teasing me I'll begin to wish I had let you die when you had typhoid fever. We spent a lot of money for doctors' bills."

There it was. It was out. I didn't know then, as a kid, that this was a "Don't exist" message, but I did know that I felt sad and angry and helpless.

As I thought further about this, I realized that Papa's avoiding me by spending all of his time with his hobbies, and by never talking to me about anything personal, was also a "Don't exist" message.

Now the pieces began to fit together. What about my response to this injunction? Did I respond with, "I'll show you if it kills me?" What does that mean? Then I began to think about my life. The way I worked for grades in high school and college. No social life, just work. High grades, yes. The highest average in the sophomore class at Swarthmore College, and an award for it ($600, which seemed like $6,000 then). Fun? No. Work? Yes. Success in grades? Yes. What was I trying to prove by studying all the time and never going to parties? By not taking part in the social life about me?

"I'll show you if it kills me." That was it. "I'll show you if it kills me." I'll show you, Papa, that I'm so good that you will have to notice me. But he didn't. He wasn't able to say anything personal; he just continued to talk about the weather.

I began to see that my need to work compulsively was rooted in my desire to please my father and win his attention. I was vaguely becoming aware of a desire to give this up, but I didn't know how.

The next morning, about 6:30 A.M., I walked out of my room into the yard. There was Bob, sitting with his feet in the swimming pool. "Bob," I said, "I got a 'Don't exist' injunction from my father." He looked at me and smiled appreciatively.

As I thought further about other injunctions during the next few days, I realized that I had received the following additional ones from my father: "Don't be close," "Don't show your feelings," "Don't have feelings," "Don't belong," "Don't trust," and "Don't have fun."

From Mother I got, "Don't show your feelings to Father." Mother gave me a straight "Do exist" message, in contrast to the "Don't exist" one from my father; but I chose to be most affected by the one from Papa, chose so early that I don't remember when.

The next morning Mary began to talk about rackets. What she said was so clearly stated and to the point that I began to be in touch with a new level of awareness. This was my first introduction to the concept of rackets, and I began to organize my thinking to include the possibility that I, too, might have some, though I didn't know what they were.

I kept very careful notes. Here are some of the things that Mary said that struck me with particular force. I want to share them with you.

"Rackets begin early. Certainly by the age of five or six. By that time children have experienced most of all of the emotions: anger, sadness, depression, for example. The racket is picked up from things the parents say or do, such as, 'Smile through adversity.' The child grows up feeling that he has to find adversity so he can smile through it. Or the child has an angry father and believes that the way to be a man is to be angry. So when he is supposed to be close, he is angry.

"Some of these rackets," Mary said, "have magical thinking underlying them, such as the idea that if I am unhappy enough, people will be sorry for me.

"The impetus to the formation and maintenance of a racket," Mary continued, "is that the parents stroke it in, either negatively or positively. An example is the mother who says to her child, who is going to the first grade, 'Don't be scared.' The child comes back scared. His mother anxiously reassures him. He learns from her to be frightened and anxious. These feelings become a racket—a scared or be afraid or anxiety racket.

"Rackets are also established as a response to parent injunctions. For example, a mother says to her child in a sudden burst of anger, 'If it hadn't been for you, I wouldn't have had to marry your father.' The usual racket response to such a 'Don't exist' injunction is sadness or depression or despair.

"One way that we maintain rackets is to go out of the present into the past or future. For example, a person who has an anxiety racket might say, 'I gave a talk in Philadelphia last week, and if I had only said such and such, everything would be fine' or 'I'm going to give a talk in New York tomorrow and I know I'll forget to say something important.' The person with a racket always looks for some way of justifying it.

"One of the best ways to stay out of a racket," Mary said, "is to stay in the 'here and now.' Get into your Adult, and give up all of the 'if onlys' and the 'what ifs.'"

Bob interjected: "People often believe that they aren't in charge of their feelings, and so can't change their rackets, can't replace them with good feelings. 'I was born that way,' they say. In this way they cop out. A second copout is, 'My unconscious makes me feel so and so.' Well, if you aren't responsible for your unconscious, who is? It's *your* unconscious."

What is *my* racket? I wondered. Well, I wasn't so sure I had a racket at first. But anyway, I kept an open mind, and considered it. What *are* some of the rackets? I asked myself as I drank a Coke while sitting at the edge of the pool during a break. What can I identify in this list that applies to me? Anger? Yes. Depression? Yes. Anxiety? Yes.

Ever since childhood I had been angry at my father—angry that he didn't pay any attention to me for my accomplishments, even more angry that he didn't pay attention to me for me. Yet, from the time I left home many years ago, he made no demands on me, nor did he interfere in my life in any way. The continuance of my feelings of anger in the absence of a present cause had no current value, nor did it lead to any constructive action. Obviously, I thought, this is an anger racket.

As I was thinking about this, my roommate, John, came along. "I have an anger racket," I said. "I never knew it before, because I don't express anger, or rarely express it. I repress it." "How come?" John asked. "I don't know," I said. "I can feel the anger inside of me." Then I realized that I had gotten a "Don't show your feelings" injunction from my father, and from my mother, too, as far as expressing feelings or anger toward either one of them was concerned. So expressing feelings, especially anger, was taboo. "I got a 'Don't show your feelings' injunction," I exclaimed. "That's why I don't show my anger. But it's there, and I waste a lot of energy holding it back. It's about time I got rid of it."

I also made contact with another set of feelings that felt to me like a racket. This was anxiety—anxiety about being accepted; anxiety about being an outsider; anxiety about whether or not I would receive approval for what I did. I knew these feelings were not justified by facts, yet I felt them anyway.

Another set of rackety feelings of which I gradually became aware was a series of recurrent depressions that I had experienced during certain periods in my life. Depression when there was nothing to be depressed about—in fact, when everything was going well. A feeling of depression which began by my father's ignoring me, and by saying such things as, "If you keep on teasing me for a bicycle, I'll begin to wish I had let you die when you had typhoid fever."

As I thought about this in the new language I was learning, I was astonished at the ease with which I was able to understand the significance of these feelings, feelings that I had been vaguely aware of before but never understood so clearly.

After lunch Bob went on to explain games. As I listened, I began to wonder what games I play. Since the whole subject was fairly new to me, and since games are played out of awareness anyway, I had no idea. As the workshop progressed, I began to understand games better and came to the conclusion that one of my games is called Stupid. I used to play it at the workshop by asking Mary where the next meeting was, as if I had read the very explicit directions that she had put up on the door and didn't understand them. She would say, "Did you read the directions I put up on the door?" I would say, "No." She would say, "Well, look at them." I didn't know this was a game then, but I always felt stupid after I asked the question, which feeling was the payoff of the game. I appreciate Mary's refusing to play it with me, because that's how I was able to pick it up.

Another thing I did at the workshop, which I gradually became aware of, was to misplace my things—pens, notebooks, my glasses. Then I would ask other people if they had seen them, hoping that they would look for them with me, or—even better—that they would find them for me. I remember how upset I used to be when it would be time to start a meeting and I couldn't find my notebook.

As I sit here writing, Corlis says she has a fantasy about me. I say, "Don't tell me, help me write this book." She says, "This will." I say, "OK, tell me your fantasy."

"I can see you as a little boy," Corlis said, "working very hard to get good marks and please Papa, while you depended on Mama to take care of the nonessentials, such as finding your books and notebooks, gloves, hat, and so forth, and getting you off to school in one piece."

"That's exactly right," I said, laughing, and then seriously, "I don't need Mama to do that for me anymore."

Just before the session closed, Bob said, "In summary, we see that each person contains three ego states: Parent, Adult, and Child. The irrational Child in the parent gives an injunction to his/her child (offspring) and his/her Parent ego state gives a counterinjunction.

"On the basis first of the injunctions, and later the counterinjunctions, the child makes an early decision about how he is going to react to his parents' treatment of him, and this decision is the basis for the development of the first act of his life script. He supports the script with rackets and the rackets with games.

"During the process, he collects brown stamps [which is the TA name for injustices] and keeps them in books. He collects enough brown stamps so that he can have a tantrum and not feel bad. As he grows into adulthood he collects more brown stamps, and in consequence behaves in such a way that his boss fires him. Then he gets married and collects more brown stamps from his wife. Finally he has enough books of brown stamps to justify a free divorce, i.e., one without guilt. In this way, he maintains his script.

"By this time he has collected enough books of brown stamps to get fired from three jobs. Finally he has enough brown stamps to justify a free suicide. One day he is shortchanged by the toll collector at the entrance to a bridge. He drives to the middle of the bridge, gets out of his car, and jumps over—to his death. This is the fatal outcome to the injunction, 'Don't exist.' Collecting and hoarding brown stamps are the steps on the way.

"What can we do about this?" Bob asked. "The patient," he continued, "needs to make a redecision. And it must be *his* redecision, not the therapist's. As in the case of a couple I worked with. The redecision was whether to be close or not to be close. They decided not to be close. Then they were distant without playing Uproar and other games. In a month, after declining not to be close, they came back and said, 'We are tired of not being close. We want to learn to be close.'

"One of the effects of the 'Don't be' ['Don't exist'] injunction from Mother, for example, is that the child gets the idea that 'Mother will love me if I am dead' and forgets that he'll be dead and won't be around to know it, even if she would. We hear this over and over again with children, as in the case of the little boy who says to his mother, 'You'll come to my funeral and cry,' without realizing that death is death. This is an irrational solution.

"Another alternative solution to 'I'll kill myself' [response to the 'Don't exist' injunction] is 'I'll run away.' Even if it isn't done in actuality, the thought of it helps the child to survive. Then later, as he grows older, he acts out this early decision. He leaves one school after another and one job after another, and this becomes an important factor in determining the character of his life script."

I thought, I never had this alternative solution. On the contrary, I always stick to what I'm doing till it's finished. This is my way of handling the "Don't exist" injunction. Come hell or high water, I'll finish. I'll show you if it kills me. Well, it hasn't yet, I thought, and it's not going to from now on, that's for sure, because I've made a redecision about that.

"The script," Bob said, "is how the child follows out the injunctions. The child establishes in a careful way how he will do this. This is often done by picking out some hero in a fairy tale or nursery rhyme or story and imitating that hero. For example, the girl whose father didn't love her decides 'I will become a sleeping beauty and then father will love me.'

"Or the girl who imitates Cinderella and keeps waiting for the fairy godmother, but goes right on sweeping the hearth. There is no magical ending in real life.

"Humpty Dumpty was the character that one person in another workshop liked best. He liked all the king's soldiers and all the king's men rushing in to put Humpty Dumpty together again. He didn't realize that Humpty Dumpty was an egg and couldn't be put together again.

"We are impressed," Bob said, "with the repetition of the *first act*, over and over again, as the person proceeds to follow out his life script. Like the girl whose husband left her. She was depressed and said she would stay depressed till her husband came back. She cried when she didn't get what she wanted.

"I asked her," Bob said, "when was the first time she had cried and cried when she didn't get what she wanted? She replied that when she was a little girl her father got her the wrong doll. She cried and cried, and then her father went right down and got her the doll she wanted.

"Her husband got tired of her crying this way repeatedly and left. He didn't come back.

"Eric Berne thought," Bob said "that after analysis of ego states, transactions, games, rackets, and scripts, the patient was finished. But there are patients in Transactional Analysis who have been in therapy for four years and with whom all of these things have been done, who say they still don't feel well. So we have been looking for ways to intervene.

"We are impressed with the power of positive strokes. We teach people how to get and give positive strokes. Also, we go back in the patient's history as far as possible and look for the first decision, the early decision. Then we work for a redecision. We feel the redecision is the most important item to get to. In order to get to it, however, there must be a previous 'gut' understanding of why the parents behaved as they did. The early decision is made by the child in response to the way he is treated by his parents, and is absolutely essential to his survival.

"This must be understood first, before the redecision is made, and in a sense, for the patient to be released to be free he needs to understand and forgive his parents. Take for example Henry, a man in an earlier workshop who had been goaded and pushed by his father, and who later became valedictorian of his class in high school, but who had never received approval from his father.

" 'Did anyone ever praise you as a kid?' we asked.

" 'No, never,' he said.

"We asked him to imagine that his father was sitting on the empty chair in front of him and suggested that he tell his father how he felt about him as a kid. Henry said that he wanted to be praised by him, and that when his father didn't do this he felt sad, depressed, and underneath this, angry. As he talked about this, he expressed these feelings of sadness and depression, and then finally his feelings of anger. We asked him to switch roles and be his father. When he was playing his father's role he said that no one had ever praised *him,* and he didn't know how to praise anyone. Then when he switched back to his own role Henry said to his father, 'You can't praise me, you don't know how. No one ever praised you. I understand now where you are, and I can forgive you.'

"This is very important, this forgiveness.

"It is best to finish this Gestalt procedure when the patient gives up being a child and feels equal to his parents. But this cannot be accomplished by words alone—not by all the words in the world. What is needed is a deep emotional re-experiencing of the early scene, in which the patient contacts and expresses the deep and primitive feelings which he originally felt but never expressed, and may never even have recognized.

"Verbal comprehension helps, but it is not enough in and of itself. Radical personality change is most likely to occur, in my experience, when the patient both understands his inner problems and present predicament and experiences them emotionally in depth."

It was time to break for the night.

The next morning we assembled in the Gouldings' living room again. I won't say anything about what happened in the workshop that morning, except what applied directly to me. One of the girls in the group worked on her feelings about her father and was getting out a lot of anger in a Gestalt double-chair fantasy experience. I began to think about my father. I had already gotten out a lot of anger at him when I had worked with Jim Simkins at Esalen, but this began to resonate the deeper feelings that were still there.

"I would like to work on my father," I said. Bob said OK, so I put my father on a chair and started to tell him how I felt. "After all, Father," I said, "I know you can't show feelings to anyone, not just me. But I hurt. I hurt. I hurt. It doesn't help me that you can't show feelings to my brother or my sister or to mother. I want you to notice me. Pay attention to me. Pay attention to me." The last time I said this, I was yelling as loud as I could. I could feel my anger rising. Then suddenly I went limp, thinking of the futility of it, and began to cry. "After all," I said, "what good is it going to do to keep on being angry all my life."

. Bob looked at me and said, "Dick, did you ever say good-bye to your father?"

I looked at him, not quite understanding what he had in mind. "What do you mean?" I asked.

"I mean, did you ever say a final good-bye to him, and then bury him in fantasy?"

"No," I said.

"Would you like to?" Bob asked.

"Yes."

"Well, put him on the chair in front of you in fantasy,

and say whatever you haven't said to him—anything that you want to—and then say good-bye to him, and bury him."

I was immersed in deep feelings. Sad feelings. I started slowly. "I always wanted you to be close to me, to put your arms around me. You never did . . . Well . . . it's not quite true that you never did. When I was a little kid about three years old you did take me out on double-runner ice skates, on the mill pond, and you put the skates on me, and I stood up holding onto your leg. You did reach down and hold on to me so I wouldn't fall. That felt so good, Father. I trusted you. I felt you were the most powerful father in the world. I *liked* that. I felt so safe. And then when you took me out riding on the handlebars of your bicycle. I was so small you just picked me up and put me in the basket on the handlebars. I wasn't afraid at all. It seemed very high up there, but I wasn't afraid. That's what I'm going to remember, Father. Those good times, when I felt close to you. I feel close now.

"Now I'm ready to say good-bye. I am going to say good-bye to you while we are both standing on the bow of my sailboat, with our arms on each other's shoulders. I know you loved boats, Father, and I know you would love my boat. I want to tell you about it. It is a beautiful Fiberglas boat. Light green deck, pure white sides, a small cabin and the most beautiful tall aluminum mast and white sail in the world. They look like clouds, Father, the jenny and the mainsail, bulging in the wind, with the blue sky and the white clouds above them. Can you feel the boat leaping gently forward on the waves? Can you feel the sails tugging? And can you see in the distance the far horizon with the waves breaking?

"You would have loved this, Father. I wish you were alive to be here with me." I could feel the tears beginning to come into my eyes, and a catch in my throat. I began to sob convulsively. Full, deep, unrestrained sobs. The tears were flowing and dropping to the floor. My nose was dripping. I turned to one of the men in the group and said, "Will you be my father, I want to hug you." I was just about to hug him when Bob intervened. "No, don't do that," he said. "Don't touch anybody while you are working. It will only make it last longer." I turned away and continued sobbing.

Time passed. I don't know how much. I lay on the floor and sobbed and sobbed and sobbed.

I pushed myself up on one arm, and then sat with my legs curled beside me on the floor. I didn't hear anything. Not a sound. I didn't see anything either. I didn't see Bob or Mary or any of the group members. I just saw my father sitting on the floor beside me. I looked into his eyes for a long time, without saying a word. Blue-gray, and steady. I saw the determined cut of his cheek and chin, and his gray sideburns and goatee. I saw his strong arms and large hands and big chest. Strong from many years of rugged work on the farm when he was a child. I looked into his eyes again. They were clear and firm. "I will not ask for pity," they said. "I will take the responsibility for me on my own. I will do what I can for Mama and for Walter and for Frances and for you, and I will not complain. I will do the best I can, and that is all I can do. I'll rest then." His eyes were clear and steady, and he held his head high and proud.

"Good-bye, Father," I said. "I love you."

"Now bury him," Bob said.

I got up and dug a grave in pantomime in the living room floor. I bent down, I pushed the spade deep into the earth. I tossed the earth beside the grave. When it was deep enough and wide enough and long enough, I picked my father up and lowered him gently into the grave. I took off my sweater and laid it gently over his face. Then I shoveled the earth back into the grave again. After it was all back it made a little mound. I stood looking at it.

"Stamp it down," Mary said. I took my feet and gently but firmly pushed the earth back into place.

As I did, I felt a lightness begin to develop in my chest, and my head felt clearer.

Gradually I began to become aware that there were other people in the room. I looked around. I saw understanding. I saw love. Marion, one of the group members who was sitting on the floor beside me, a middle-aged woman, was quietly sobbing. I went over to her and took her hands.

"I was with you," she said, "all the time."

It was time for lunch. Everyone left the room but me. I sat quietly for a while, just experiencing my feelings. A sense of sadness, a sense of quietness, a sense of peace.

This gestalt with my father took place six years ago. Ever since then I have not had any feelings of anger toward him. They have been replaced by warm feelings and the memories of the good things that happened between him and me.

In his own way, I now know that he wanted the best for me, which is why he emphasized studying hard. The academic life had been his dream—one which he had given up in the mistaken belief that he could not have it and still support his family.

This final release of anger toward my father, and reconciliation with him, freed my energy in many directions. I remember the ensuing days as some of the most carefree and joyous of my life.

# CHAPTER
## 6

## *How My Patients Changed*

When I returned to New York, I was eager to incorporate into my work with groups and individuals the new techniques I had learned in the workshops I had attended during the past several years on the West Coast. These techniques were, as you know, Gestalt Therapy, Transactional Analysis and nonverbal communication methods. I had learned by this time how to use these techniques as the therapeutic occasion required. When Gestalt Therapy was indicated I used that; when TA was more appropriate, I used TA; when nonverbal communication methods were more useful, I used them.

A striking instance of the effect of nonverbal "eye-to-eye" contact occurred in the case of Paul, a social worker in a group I was leading at the William Alanson White Psychoanalytic Institute. I had noticed that Paul never looked directly at anybody, and I called this to his attention. He said he had a squint in his right eye, and that he never looked directly at anyone because he thought it would embarrass him. I asked him if he would pick out someone in the room and look directly into the eyes of that person for one minute. Paul picked a pretty girl, Grace.

After one minute I asked him to ask Grace how she felt about his looking at her. She said she had never made as good or direct a contact with him before. This amazed him.

I then asked him if he would go to each person in the group and look directly into his or her eyes for thirty seconds. He went to each of the eleven other people in the group, and the results were universally the same.

After he finished, I asked Paul how he felt. He said, with much surprise, "Great! Dr. Abell, I never expected to be able to look directly at a person, and have him look directly at me, without being embarrassed."

I have found, in many cases, the direct experiencing and the taking a risk (which this involves) is worth hours of verbalization (that is, talking about it).

Another example of the effectiveness of dealing directly with what a person is feeling in the "here and now" occurs frequently when new members are introduced into a therapy group. When I ask them how they feel, they frequently reply, "Scared." Then I say, "Will you go to each person in the group and say, 'I'm scared.'?" By the time they have gone halfway around and have received the responses of the group members, they are feeling greatly relieved.

This reminds me of an amusing incident concerning a woman in one of my groups who was afraid to speak up. I asked her if she would be willing to go around the group and say to each member, "I'm afraid to speak up." She was feeling so good when she finished, I asked her to make a speech to the group. She did, with obvious surprise and pleasure at the ease with which she spoke. As a matter of fact, she got so turned on that it was difficult for me to turn her off. In the end, everybody was laughing, and so was she.

## GEORGE: I'M NOT OK–YOU'RE NOT OK

An instance showing the effectiveness of combining Gestalt Therapy and TA is the case of George, a thirty-five-year-old mathematics teacher who told me that before he came to see me he had been to nine other therapists; some of whom he said, and I knew, were the best in the field. This gave me pause for a few brief moments of thought, but I took him on anyway. He came to see me because he was depressed, angry, and isolated. His existential position was "I'm Not OK–You're Not OK." I saw George both privately and in group therapy for two years prior to the incident that I am going to describe, and in this period had used only psychoanalytic techniques. I had urged him to do Gestalt double-chair work with his father, but he had refused, saying that this was not the way to do therapy, none of his other therapists had ever done therapy like that with him, and he wasn't going to do it with me.

During this time I had been working with his "transference" reactions to me, in approved psychoanalytic fashion. By "transference" is meant a reaction in which the patient transfers to the analyst a feeling or emotion that he had toward some key figure in the past. For example, George had feelings of anger toward his father which had not been resolved, and he transferred these feelings to me.

An instance illustrating this occurred one time when George was going around the group and asking for something that he wanted from each member. When he came to me he said, "Doc, I would like you to let me use you as a punching bag." "I won't do that," I said. "If you punch me, I'll punch you back." "What do you mean?" he said. "That's what I'm paying you for." "That's not the way I make my living, George, by being a punching bag. As a matter of fact, I've never done anything to make you angry at me, have I?" "If you mean," George said, "that you

haven't been harsh with me, or said unpleasant things, no."
"You aren't angry at me, George," I said. "You are angry at somebody else. Who is it?" "I'm angry at my father," he said, "if that's what you had in mind." "Yes, that's what I did have in mind," I said. We had gone over and over George's unhappy relationship with his father, and he had told me about how his father had beaten his mother and his sister and refused to allow George to do any of the things that he really wanted to do. This "talking about" had not resolved George's feelings of anger toward me at all.

"George," I said, "you have been talking about the anger you feel at your father for over a year, and it really hasn't helped much. How about using one of the new techniques I learned on the West Coast now. Put your father on this chair in front of you, in fantasy, and tell him exactly how you feel about him. Then play the role of your father and answer back to yourself, and keep on with this dialogue until you have gotten out all the feelings toward your father that you want to."

"Doc," George said again, "I've been to nine therapists before I came to you, and none of them did this. I won't do it."

"Did it ever occur to you that this may be one of the reasons you didn't get over these angry feelings?" I asked, and let the matter drop.

George continued to see me. He was always finding fault with me, telling me what I was doing that was wrong. This didn't help him feel better, as I knew it wouldn't. But explanations and interpretations were of no avail—he was in an anger racket.

Finally one day George came to see me feeling deeply depressed. "I don't know what I'm going to do, Doc," he said. "I feel life isn't worthwhile anymore. If things don't get better . . . you know, Doc, I'm thinking of suicide. These thoughts come into my head. Sometimes I just lie in bed thinking of how I'll do it."

"Obviously the usual therapeutic methods aren't helping you, I said. "Are you willing to try some of the newer methods now?"

With his back to the wall, and nothing to lose, since he was contemplating suicide anyway, George finally said, "All right, Doc, I'll do it. What shall I do?"

"Sit in this chair and face this other empty chair. As you sit there, imagine that your father is sitting in the chair in front of you, and tell him in the present tense how you feel about him and what he did to you. You can be any age you want to, but speak in the present tense."

"I'll be the age I am now," George said. "Pop, I want you to love me, but you don't ever show me that you do. You don't tell me that you care about me. You don't hit me like you do Mom and Sis, but it frightens me when you hit them. I'm always afraid I'll be next. Why do you hit Mom? Mom is so nice to me. If it hadn't been for Mom, I don't know what would have happened to me. I don't want you to hit Mom, Pop. It makes me mad." (His voice sounded more pleading than angry.)

I put a pillow on his father's chair and said, "You don't sound mad, George. You sound as if you are pleading with your father. Say, 'It makes me mad when you hit Mom' ten times, and hit this pillow every time you say 'mad.' I'll keep count."

"It makes me mad when you hit Mom." Weak voice and weak hit.

"Say it louder," I said.

"It makes me mad when you hit Mom." Still weak.

"Louder," I urged.

"It makes me MAD when you hit Mom."

"That's better. Say it even louder."

"It makes ME MAD WHEN YOU hit Mom." George hit the pillow hard that time.

"Say it again, as loud as you can, and hit the pillow even harder."

"IT MAKES ME MAD WHEN YOU HIT MOM,"

George yelled, and hit the pillow really hard.

Then George exploded, kicked over the chair, knocked the pillow to the floor, jumped on top of it and started beating it. Then he began pushing the pillow all over the floor, beating it and yelling, "I hate you, Pop. I hate you, I hate you. Why can't you let me do what I want? Why do you laugh at me when I read books? Why do you keep me from playing the piano? I hate you, I hate you."

After about five minutes of this violent activity, George stopped, and lay panting on the floor. Then he got up and went to his chair. For several minutes he sat with his head in his hands, saying nothing. Then he began to cry, with deep, long, convulsive sobs.

That was the beginning of George's getting in touch with his real feelings of grief and anger. All of the "talking about" in the world does not produce this kind of deep response. Gestalt "double-chair dialogue with key figures" does almost routinely. And without such deep release there is no deep character change, no letting go of the "hanging-on bite." "Talking about" can go on for years and years, but without the expression of such "gut" reactions, profound change does not occur.

Fritz Perls says that the patient "explodes" out of the impasse.[1] George had had his first explosion.

The work that George began in this session was continued in a twelve-hour marathon (or "minithon") the following Saturday.

## TWELVE-HOUR MARATHON

There were twenty people in this marathon, which was held in Wainwright House in Rye, New York, a beautiful replica of a French château overlooking an estuary of Long Island Sound. The rooms were large and spacious, carpeted with Oriental rugs, with windows looking out over an expansive lawn which ran to the water's edge.

This impressive estate is dedicated to the exploration of new approaches and to the development of the Human Potential Movement.

George was one of the group members gathered in the library. As usual, he had been reluctant to come to the marathon and, in an unconscious attempt to avoid it, had engaged in a lively game of Why Not, Yes But in the last group session. When I refused to continue to play this game with him, he decided to take a risk and come.

I am going to show how I used the methods of TA, Gestalt Therapy and nonverbal communication in this marathon in a particularly dramatic episode with George, in which he made changes in his feelings about his real father and his own Critical Parent, and the group members, particularly several of the women.

George had always had a problem with women. Even when he overcame some of his bashfulness and was able to invite one for a date, he always did something to prevent himself from getting close to her, which led to his subsequent rejection. But he was never able to determine exactly what he did, since it was out of his awareness.

George, of course, had received many "heavy" injunctions, such as: "Don't exist," "Don't be you," "Don't belong," "Don't be close," "Don't be important," "Don't trust," and "Don't make it." You will notice, as you read the verbatim transcript which follows, how deeply George was still enmeshed in these injunctions at this time and how unaware he was of the fact that this was true.

George had an angry and a depressed racket. These rackets kept him in the existential position: "I'm Not OK—You're Not OK." It is no wonder that he found it difficult to change, since most of his life had been spent being angry at people, distrusting them, and avoiding any close contacts. He was depressed living alone in his room with his fantasies, but that seemed safer than venturing into a world which was terrifying to his Adapted Child. He felt that if he made a move toward real pleasure, he would be destroyed. When he began therapy with me, his options were becoming more and more limited, so that he increasingly fantasized the ultimate option—suicide.

The games which forwarded George's rackets were: Now I've Got You; You Son of a Bitch; Kick Me; Why Don't You, Yes But; and Wooden Leg.

His early decision was to "work hard, be miserable, and avoid closeness." His Adapted Child fantasy was of a beautiful Princess who would come along and turn him from a Frog (loser) into a Prince (winner). This magical event, of course, never happened.

George hoped to find his Princess in the group in this marathon (as he does in every group meeting he is in), and he successively picked three of the prettiest girls in the room for his partner in the exercises.

The following one-hour segment of the marathon occurred during the third hour. During the first two hours the group members had been formulating the contracts that they wanted to fulfill during the marathon. George's contract was that he would work on being closer to the women in the group.

This is what happened:

I began the third hour by introducing a nonverbal exercise involving touching. "Mill around the room among each other," I said, "and as you go by each person, touch or shake his hand in such a way as to show how you are feeling about him. Do not talk. Continue until I tell you to stop."

As we all milled around I noticed that George approached one of the girls, and as he took her hand she winced. The same thing happened with the next girl whose hand he shook.

After about five minutes I asked everyone to pick partners, stand back to back, and have a conversation without talking. George went immediately to Laura, an attractive, outgoing girl. The other couples had a great time enjoying the encounters, but George was rough with Laura, and she objected. He twisted Laura's hand behind her back, and pushed her toward the wall. I heard Laura say, "George, you're hurting me!" She broke away from him and went to the side of the room, where she watched the other couples.

When the exercise was over, I asked everyone to sit down and said, "Now let's have some playback. Will you each tell your partner how you felt about what he did and about what you did, and what you communicated to each other in this exercise."

The following dialogue is from the transcript of a tape I made during the marathon:

GEORGE: I'd like the two women I had the last exercise with to tell me their reactions to me, because I feel acutely uncomfortable about what happened. I have a feeling that some of my basic attitudes are involved in what they experienced toward me, as well as what you experienced with me, Laura. I didn't realize, Laura, how sharp your reaction would be. The more vivid expression to use would be that I turned you off completely, so that we stopped somewhere in the middle of the exercise and watched the others proceed.

DOCTOR: Well, how did you turn Laura off?

GEORGE: Do you want to describe your feelings again, Laura?

LAURA: Uh—I had gone through this exercise before, and George never had. But I felt like I was being pushed against the wall. You were pushing very hard, with tremendous pressure, George. (LAURA *turned to* GEORGE *as she said this, and her voice showed anger and irritation.*) I tried to get you to relax, but you refused. I just felt like stopping, 'cause I felt you were just grabbing me, and I didn't feel that this is the way the exercise was meant to be carried out. I felt you were letting out some aggression on me that had nothing to do with me.

DOCTOR: Do you have any playback, George?

GEORGE:   Well, first, I'm not totally surprised that you thought I was very aggressive. But your telling me I didn't get anything out of this is your projection, Laura. As a matter of fact . . .

LAURA:   Oh, I didn't say that you didn't get anything out of it. I said how *I* felt. What you got out of it was probably totally different. I'm the one that broke it off.

TED:   Did you want to be aggressive, George?

GEORGE:   I don't know that I can answer *what I wanted* to be. I felt compelled to be aggressive.

JAN:   By what?

GEORGE:   Some inner drive. Something, something was driving me to lose control.

DOCTOR:   I want to say a word about something driving you to lose control, something you don't know anything about, like your unconscious. If *you* don't know what is driving you to lose control, who does? Whatever impulses you have are yours. You can find out what they are and be responsible for them, and I'll help you."

GEORGE *(showing some irritation):*   If what you're communicating to me is that I can develop some control over these impulses, then that's fine. Then we meet some place.

DOCTOR:   That's what I do, myself, George. Whatever I do I take the responsibility for it. If it isn't what I want to do, then I find out what's going wrong, and change it.

GEORGE:   I was overly aggressive with you, Vera, in the hand-to-hand exercise, and I know I was overly aggressive with you, Laura. I did not realize the effect this was having on you. I was disappointed when you said, "Let's stop." Very much so.

VERA:   What were you doing, George? I'm trying to imagine what you *could* do back to back with Laura that was overly aggressive.

LAURA:   I was being pushed, and there was tremendous pressure. At one time you pulled my hands behind me. (LAURA *elevated her voice and was obviously angry when she said, "hands behind me."*) I don't know if you heard me say, "You're hurting me."

BERNIE:  I heard it. *(Members of the group agree, saying,* "We heard it too.")

VERA:  You hurt me when you squeezed my hand. You squeezed so hard that you actually took the ring off my finger. (GEORGE *smiles.*)

BERNIE:  How do you feel when Vera says this, George?

GEORGE *(long pause):*  Uh—I think I wanted to overwhelm you, and the other girls, too. I wanted to let you know that I was in control.

GUERIN:  George, when Vera said that you pulled the ring off her finger you smiled. Did you know that? Do you think there is any significance to that?

GEORGE:  I think that smile is insignificant.

MARK:  I think that smile is *significant*. It shows that you liked what you did. You liked hurting the girls. You are aggressive and try to dominate. Then you get rejected, disappointed, and hurt. It happens over and over again.

DOCTOR:  What you are doing, George, you are doing because of your anger racket. At least that seems to be a part of it, to me. You are angry, and so you find ways to express it. You pick girls for this, and do something painful to them. This is an expression of your anger, and it causes the girls to reject you, over and over again. In a certain sense, I would assume you like this feeling of being rejected, perhaps because it keeps you in the same rejected feeling that you had as a kid. *(I knew GEORGE had such feelings of rejection when he was young because we had discussed this in his private therapy.)* Sometimes it seems safer to stay in the same feelings we had when we were young than to change them. Were such feelings of rejection familiar to you as a child?

GEORGE:  Yes, quite so.

DOCTOR:  So you manage to do things in the present

that keep you rejected. Then you feel unhappy, isolated, separated, just as you did as a kid.

GEORGE: Uh—it's not my feeling that I wanted to be rejected by Laura. Just the opposite. I felt attracted by you, Laura. That's why I went directly to you. I wanted to have one exercise with you. But it doesn't feel to me as if I approached you in order to be rejected.

DOCTOR: Whatever the cause is, you do get rejected often.

GEORGE: Yes.

DOCTOR: How come?

GEORGE: Because I apparently behave in such a way as to get the women to reject me.

DOCTOR: That's true.

GEORGE: That's the feedback I wanted anyway. I wanted to hear this.

DOCTOR: What did you want to hear it for?

GEORGE: So that I can learn to modify it.

DOCTOR: Terrific.

BERNIE: Do you *want* to be accepted?

GEORGE: Yes, I do.

BERNIE: Knowing that it's scary?

GEORGE: That's right. I am scared at the thought of being accepted and what that involves, but I have a craving to be accepted.

LESLIE: What would happen to you that you are so afraid of if you were accepted?

GEORGE: I am afraid of being enveloped and controlled, and that I will have to gear my moods and behavior to what the person who accepts me wants.

HARRY: Where do you get that from?

GEORGE: You mean where did it originate from? My behavior was rigidly controlled at home. Very rigidly. I've been trying to escape that all my life. I become terrified when there is a prospect that I will become controlled.

HARRY: Do you control your own behavior?

GEORGE:   Not nearly as much as I would like to.

BERNIE:   Oh, much too much for your own good.

GEORGE:   If you mean I inhibit myself too much, you are quite right.

TED:   You control yourself very rigidly with your racket. It happens continuously in our relationship, and in your relationships in our group. There is a great deal of control, and lack of spontaneity and freedom.

DOCTOR:   How would you spell that racket out, Ted?

TED *(looking at* GEORGE):   You put yourself in a situation of being rejected or being alienated in order to keep that feeling—that bad feeling in you. You do that in many ways, I've seen. You get people to want you to do something, like come here to this marathon. Then when they ask you to, and suggest ways that would make it possible, you reject them and say, "No, I'm not going to come." That happened with several marathons in the past, till we caught on to your game of Why Not, Yes But and stopped playing it with you. We got fed up with you, and stopped asking you to come. In a sense, we rejected you. Just now, from what I've seen here, you set up a situation where you were rejected by two women.

GEORGE:   Three women.

LINDA:   When you went around shaking hands, you squeezed my hand so hard that the stone in my ring made an impression on my hand, and it's still there.

GEORGE *(smiles).*

GUERIN *(excitedly):*   Look at that smile. *(General group reactions of exclamations and excitement.)*

HARRY:   You're getting pleasure out of hurting people, and then they reject you. What you want to do is to get pleasure from doing something nice for people, and then getting accepted by them. Obviously, this isn't going to happen if you keep on the way you are this afternoon, because you go around squeezing people's hands too hard, or making them feel uncomfortable by twisting their arms behind their back. That gives you pleasure, and that's weird. [*This puts the sadism clearly on the line for the first time.*] Whatever it is within you that makes you do that is what you want to get rid of. It's obvious to everybody that you enjoy inflicting pain, and for one reason or another, that's where your desires are really centered.

MARK: I think the same thing. Either it's time to do something about it right now, either to get up and go to some of the women and change your behavior toward them right here and now, or at least to make a step toward it, or do a gestalt and work at the root of it.

LAURA: George, are you afraid that if you got involved in a relationship with someone that you might get hurt?

GEORGE: Yes.

LAURA: So, therefore, you get great pleasure out of saying, "Aha, I hurt them and they didn't hurt me."

GEORGE: I don't know. I don't know.

GUERIN: If a woman let you beat the hell out of her, would you enjoy it?

GEORGE: No.

GUERIN: Are you sure?

GEORGE: Yeah. I'm absolutely certain of that.

DOCTOR: It is very important that you realize that you experienced pleasure and gratification when Linda said, "You squeezed my hand so hard that the stone in my ring made an impression on my hand, and it's still there." (GEORGE *looks pleased.*) You look pleased even now, when I say it. That's not the kind of thing that's good to get pleasure from. I, personally, hate sadistic behavior, George.

GEORGE *(angrily):* Doc, I can behave in any way that I want to here. I don't have to please you. I take it that this is a psychotherapeutic session in which I am allowed to reveal myself without being castigated. I'm paying for that.

DOCTOR: I'm not castigating you. I'm just pointing out some things about you that it is very important for you to become aware of.

GEORGE: You're supposed to be a doctor to me.

DOCTOR: I am being a doctor. It is important for you that I point out things that you are doing that you may not be aware of doing.

GEORGE *(still angry)*: I know what people hate. It doesn't have to be pointed out to me.

DOCTOR: Did you know that you squeezed Vera's and Linda's hand too hard, and that you hurt Laura? Did you know that they hate this?

GEORGE *(still angry)*: Yes, and I would hate it too.

DOCTOR: Then why did you do it?

GEORGE *(now somewhat confused)*: Why did I do what?

DOCTOR: Hurt Linda and Vera and Laura.

GEORGE: I didn't realize I was doing it earlier this morning. I realize it now, but I didn't realize it then.

DOCTOR: That's what I mean, George. You didn't realize you were hurting them then, when you were hurting them. That's what I mean by your not being aware of it—you're not aware of it at the time you do it.

GEORGE *(surprised)*: I guess you're right, Doc.

HARRY: But when it was pointed out to you, so that you did become aware of it, you smiled. You showed that it pleased you when you did become aware of it. Why do you get pleasure out of it when you do realize it? That's the question. What is it that gives you pleasure when you realize that you've hurt a girl?

GEORGE *(sarcastically, scornfully, and wanting to avoid the whole issue)*: I feel nothing but love.

MARK: If you feel like shit, say so.

GEORGE: I do. I'm disappointed in Dr. Abell. (GEORGE *is too insecure about this to face the problem directly, and so avoids it by deflecting his anger onto me, a common maneuver for him. Remember his saying that he wants to use me as a punching bag.*)

LINDA *(speculating)*: You think that a masculine person can't be gentle, so you have to be rough to show that you are a man. *(This hits the bull's-eye.)*

GEORGE: That's a good suggestion. *(Apparently* GEORGE *has some awareness of this, but he doesn't really comprehend its implications yet. He drops it and doesn't go on with it.)*

HELEN: There's nothing masculine about inflicting pain. I hate it when you hurt someone and then smile about it.

DOCTOR: You smiled when Guerin pointed out to you that you hurt Linda. You smiled again when I referred to the fact that you hurt Linda. And you look pleased now when I say it. It really is clear that it pleases you to hurt girls. That's what the smile says to me, and also that it pleases you to please somebody who told you in some way that it is good to hurt women. Your smile is a "gallows" smile. That is, you lose the very thing that you want—the friendship of women—by hurting them, yet you smile about it. Like the man who is going to the gallows, and then laughs about what he did that caused him to be sent to the gallows.

LINDA: What is the feeling you get with that smile? Unless you get a bad feeling about it, the smile won't evaporate.

TED: Here we are.

GUERIN: I agree with you.

DOCTOR: What is the feeling you get with the smile, George?

GEORGE *(hurt, but stoically)*: Pleasure. *(Then with a stronger voice—intent on being honest about his feelings.)* Pleasure. I felt pleasure in it.

TED: Because you felt you were strong?

GEORGE: Yes, because I felt I was strong. That's right.

LESLIE: Put the smile on the chair and talk to it.

DOCTOR *(pulls chair up opposite* GEORGE*)*: OK. Put the smile on that chair and talk to it. What do you think about that smile? *(Forty seconds of complete silence.)*

GEORGE: You're not doing me any good, smile.

DOCTOR: Sit over there on the opposite chair, and be the smile.

GEORGE: I feel great. I'm glad the girls said that I hurt them. I'm glad that Laura yelled out, "You're hurting me, George."

DOCTOR: OK. Now be George and talk to the smile. (GEORGE *shifts back into the other chair.*)

GEORGE: I'm also glad that the people here say they don't like it.

LINDA: Why? *(Pause.)*

GEORGE: Because I want them to be irritated with it. I want them to know how bad I really feel. I put you on, smile, at first, because I wanted them to see that I got a real kick out of . . . crushing . . . being overwhelming–that makes me feel strong. What I basically want is for Dr. Abell and you people here to help me not to feel weak. *(Pause for twenty seconds.)* That's it. I don't want to feel weak. *(Pause.)* And I do want to feel strong. *(Pause. Then to smile on chair):* I really don't want you to get in the way of my developing a close relationship with a woman . . . with anyone. But I have to use you, if I have no other way. But really, I don't want you to get in the way of my developing a close relationship with a woman.

TED: Say that again, George.

GEORGE: I don't want any sadistic impulse to get in my way of developing a close relationship with a woman.

DOCTOR: Say it again and say it louder.

GEORGE *(louder):* I don't want my father's sadistic impulses toward my mother to get in my way of developing a close relationship with a woman. I don't want my father's sadistic impulses toward my mother and my sister to prevent me from developing a close relationship with a woman. *I don't want it. (As* GEORGE *said, "I don't want it," he raised his voice angrily and hit the chair in front of him very hard*–bang, bang.)

DOCTOR: It would be good for you to put your father on the chair and tell him how you feel about these sadistic relationships with your mother and sister. Will you do that?

GEORGE *(long pause):*   You drove Mom into the ground. You browbeat her.... You *(voice choked with emotion)* practically made an automaton of her. You denied her ... her very humanity. You ... forced my sister to become fearful and hateful of men. And you forced me.... First I was deprived of warmth and affection and closeness with Mom, with Sally, and ... and in some way you forced me to identify with you ... and get pleasure in thinking of women as chattels—to be controlled and oppressed—and not show feelings of their own. That's what I did with Laura, Vera, and Linda today. I didn't want them to express their own feelings. I couldn't let them be themselves, just like you couldn't let Mom be herself. So I learned from you not to want them to be themselves.

DOCTOR:   Will you sit in the opposite chair now and be your father, and talk back to you?

GEORGE:   Only I have to make these things up, because my father never *said* these things to me.

DOCTOR:   OK.

GEORGE:   Shall I piece these things together?

DOCTOR:   Yes. That's a good idea.

GEORGE *(playing the role of his father):*   Uh ... your mother and your sister were always out to frustrate me ... your mother never listened to me. She never kept the house the way I wanted her to keep it. She never brought up the children the way I wanted her to bring them up. She let the children do as they pleased. When I was away, you were able to get away with whatever you pleased. It was only when I was home that I made you behave. (GEORGE's *voice is loud and clear and there is a lot of strength in it when he is taking his father's role.)* And Sally aggravated me—deliberately frustrated me. She gave me my first heart attack. I wasn't bad to them.

DOCTOR:   It's interesting that your father said, *"She*

gave me my first heart attack." *He* doesn't take the responsibility for what happens to *him*. He blames someone else—Sally.

GEORGE:   My father was that way in the extreme. He said time and time again that God was punishing him.

DOCTOR:   So talk to him again, about that.

GEORGE:   It wasn't God that punished you, Pop. You invited the results you got by your own behavior. (GEORGE *sees, probably for the first time, that his father was responsible for what happened to him, which is the beginning of his being able to see that he,* GEORGE, *is responsible for the reactions that he gets—as, for example, from women. George is going through a very significant and far-reaching breakthrough.* GEORGE *continues.*) And if Mom was as cruel and oppressive as you were, I would really be nothing today.

DOCTOR:   Say that again. *(This kind of repetition is a typical Gestalt maneuver designed to emphasize something important and to bring out feelings.)*

GEORGE:   If Mom was as cruel and oppressive as you were, I would *really* be nothing today. I would be hopeless.

DOCTOR:   Say it again.

GEORGE:   I would be *hopeless* if Mom were like you. You *(voice choking with emotion, so that he is hardly able to speak)—(recovering)* I think it's too bad that you didn't live to see the time—although it would never have happened if you had remained alive—but after you died—the warmth and sweetness that came out of Mom—was simply a wonder to see. (GEORGE'S *voice is almost disbelieving, but sympathetic.*) And I was so happy to see it. No, it wasn't God that punished you, Pop; you punished yourself. You frustrated yourself, and you frustrated all those around you. You did not allow the people around you to grow. You did not allow your children to grow. (GEORGE'S *voice becoming louder.*) You did not allow Mom to grow . . . you did not allow us to grow. You wanted to maintain a tight and rigid and absolute control over their lives ... and everything they did ... and everything they said ... and all their moods ... and their expressions. You didn't allow them to laugh, because when they laughed they expressed pleasure. You didn't allow me (GEORGE *becomes more personal*) to laugh because I was expressing pleasure, and you wanted me to keep quiet. [ *'Don't be you," "Don't show your feelings" injunctions.*]

DOCTOR:  Say that again.

GEORGE:  You didn't allow me to laugh because I was experiencing pleasure.

DOCTOR:  Say it again.

GEORGE:  You didn't allow me to laugh because I was experiencing pleasure ... and ... you didn't want me ... you wanted me to keep quiet *(voice becomes soft and sad)* and not to experience the pleasure I was feeling at the moment. You did not allow me to express any pleasure that I was feeling at any moment *(voice louder)*.

DOCTOR:  Say it again. [*I am trying to get* GEORGE *deeply into his feelings, so that he will develop enough strength and power to reject this kind of treatment.*]

GEORGE:  You did not allow me to express any pleasure that I was feeling at the moment. You did not allow me to express any feeling that I was expressing at the moment *(voice rising)*. You didn't allow me to express any pleasure. You didn't allow me to laugh *(voice loud and quick)*, you didn't allow me to listen to the music I wanted to listen to. You didn't allow me to read the books that I wanted to, because they were giving me pleasure, and *my pleasure was not your pleasure.* Your pleasure was for me to do whatever you wanted me to, and for you to maintain control over my life. And so I began to imagine that other people were treating me the same way you did. I thought no man in the world wanted me to experience any pleasures. *I believed that,* because you led me to believe it, and so I believed it. And kept on believing it *(voice choked with emotion)*.

DOCTOR:  Say that again. [*I knew by this time that*

GEORGE *was laying the groundwork for a whole change in his character and behavior. My job was to facilitate it.)*

GEORGE: I believed all my life that men were in the way of my developing a successful relationship with a woman. And I believed all my life that only if all men were dead that (GEORGE *was laboring to get this out)*— that—I'd be able to develop—a successful relationship with a woman. And I was—my father was—*(long pause).* [*When* GEORGE *said, "I was," his voice became softer and full of emotion, and when he said, "my father was" it was almost a whisper and he seemed on the verge of tears. During the long pause that followed, his head was bowed and he seemed unable to speak, he was so full of grief. The intense silence was broken by a faint cough from* HELEN.]

DOCTOR: What are your feelings about your father now?

GEORGE *(ten-second pause):* I'm—I—uh—I'm just seeing his own pathetic nature, his own helplessness.

DOCTOR: Be your father and talk to George, and tell him how pathetic and helpless you are.

GEORGE *(playing his father's role):* I had a very hard life. I lost my mother when I was twelve years old, and my father was a tyrant. You think I'm a tyrant *(then quickly, excitedly),* you think I'm a tyrant but you don't know what *my* father was like. I was a peasant on a farm, and we didn't have enough to eat. I worked sixteen hours a day. You're telling me what you didn't have—you don't know what I didn't have *(quickly, excitedly, and raising his voice).* (GEORGE *suddenly switched back into his own role and raised his voice to a yell.)* JUST BECAUSE YOU SUF-FERED DEPRIVATION IN YOUR LIFE, WHAT IS YOUR PLEASURE IN DEPRIVING ME? [*When* GEORGE *said "just because" he hit the chair in front of him hard twice, showing his sudden anger—which now, for the first time, is coming out in full bloom. This is what Freud called the "cathartic experience," the reliving in all its intensity of an original experience, and what Fritz Perls referred to as an "explosion" into authenticity.*] (GEORGE *continues.*) I KNOW THAT YOU DIDN'T HAVE THE OPPORTUNITIES THAT I HAVE–I KNOW THAT. *(There is anger, desperation, and vexation in* GEORGE'S *voice.)* BUT WHY CAN'T I ENJOY LIFE BECAUSE YOU DIDN'T ENJOY IT IN THE PAST? *(Voice strong and questioning, pleading and also assertive.)* WHY CAN'T I HAVE MY OWN LIFE JUST BECAUSE YOU DIDN'T HAVE THE ONE YOU WANTED? [GEORGE *is yelling and getting into his own power, which is absolutely essential for a breakthrough.*] WHAT HAVE I GOT TO DO WITH YOUR PAST LIFE? [GEORGE *is not only talking to his father, in fantasy, but his own internalized Critical Parent.*]

DOCTOR:   Show how you feel about your father by wringing that towel. Show how you feel about your father.

GEORGE *(takes towel in his hands and looks at it):* So you're—you're the overwhelming character that's going to crush the life out of me, Pop—huh? YOU OWN MY LIFE? *(Beginning to wring the towel.)* YOU DON'T OWN MY LIFE ANYMORE, POP. [GEORGE *shows determination and emotion, and is at the point of redecision concerning his father's effect on him.*] YOU DON'T OWN MY LIFE *(yelling).* There's no edict of yours that I have to obey. [*Redecision.*] I DIDN'T HURT YOUR LIFE. I DIDN'T CAUSE YOUR MISERY. YOU CAUSED YOUR OWN MISERY. OR SOMEBODY ELSE DID, BUT NOT I. AND I DON'T HAVE TO REMAIN MISERABLE–I DON'T HAVE TO KEEP MYSELF MISERABLE–[GEORGE *is owning his own part in his own misery for the first time.*] BECAUSE YOU WANT ME TO BE MISERABLE. I'M NOT GOING TO KEEP YOU HAPPY BY BEING MISERABLE. [*This is breaking an injunction, the reverse of a gallows smile or laugh.*] AND I'M NOT GOING TO BELIEVE THAT OTHER MEN WANT ME TO BE MISERABLE. [*Redecision.*] I'M NOT GOING TO BELIEVE THAT OTHER MEN WANT ME

TO BE MISERABLE. I'M NOT GOING TO BELIEVE
THAT OTHER MEN WANT ME TO BE MISERABLE
*(pause).*

TED *(speaking in an intense and low voice):* George,
show how you feel about your father with that towel.
Show how you feel. Wring the towel.

VERA *(as* GEORGE *looks at the towel and does nothing
with it):* He's still not sure. You're not sure that you want
to kill your father off. How do you feel?

GEORGE *(throwing the towel to the floor):* I discarded
him. I discarded him.

LESLIE:   He's still alive. You left him alive.

VERA:   He's alive.

HELEN:   Every bit as powerful as he was.

TED:   How do you feel about it? How do you feel
about it?

LESLIE:   Still alive, and he'll get you.

DOCTOR:   Wring his neck.

VERA:   He'll get you again tomorrow. Don't you
want to kill him?

GEORGE:   No, I don't want to kill him, I want to kill
his tyranny.

DOCTOR:   You don't have to kill your father. It's
better that you don't. Kill off the bad things that he did to
you. Kill off the tyranny.

LESLIE:   The towel is his tyranny.

GEORGE *(who has been listening to all of this care-
fully picks the towel up and holds it loosely in his hands.
Suddenly he begins to wring it violently):* I am destroying
your tyranny. I AM DESTROYING YOUR STRAN-
GLEHOLD. SEE. *(He wrings the towel with great force,
the effort showing in his voice, as he speaks while wring-
ing the towel.)* SEE, YOUR STRANGLEHOLD–I'M
KILLING IT, I'M GETTING IT OUT OF MY LIFE.
THERE GOES YOUR STRANGLEHOLD–AWAY–
OUT. *(*GEORGE *throws the towel onto the floor.)*

LESLIE:   Is it dead?

TED:   Is it gone?

LESLIE:   I think it's still alive.

TED:   Get the tyranny—there it is. Strangle it. Kill it. *(Several sighs around in the group that are audible in the silence. After a moment, George picks up the towel.)*

GEORGE:   You see, I'm doing this to your tyranny. I'm not going to—NEVER AGAIN WILL I GRAB THE HANDS OF A WOMAN AND DO THIS TO HER *(wringing the towel).* [*Redecision.*] I'M DOING THIS TO YOUR OPPRESSION. *YOUR OPPRESSION.* YOURS. I'm not doing this to Mom *(in quick succession)* but to you, TO YOU, TO YOU. NEVER AGAIN TO ANOTHER WOMAN. *NEVER.*

DOCTOR:   How do you feel, George?

GEORGE   *(breathing hard):* I'm through. But—but— I—uh—I think Pop still wants me to hate my mother like he did.

DOCTOR:   Talk to him.

GEORGE:   You—you—want me to hate Mom like you did. You want me to hate Sally like you did. You want me to be your ally. I had to be your friend. I had to hate my sister, like you did. I had to beat my sister, like you did. I had to hate her, like you did. Like you did. LIKE YOU DID. WHY DO I HAVE TO HATE THEM LIKE YOU DID? *(breathing hard, almost panting).* ALL MY LIFE I WANTED TO EXPRESS MY LOVE FOR SALLY AND YOU PREVENTED ME. I HAD TO HATE HER, LIKE YOU DID. I HAD TO BE YOUR ALLY. OUT WITH YOUR TYRANNY. *I'M NOT YOUR ALLY* [*Redecision.*] I'M NOT YOUR ALLY. I'M NOT AN ALLY TO YOUR TYRANNY. I'LL NOT BE OPPRESSIVE *(wrings towel hard).* Ah-uh-rr *(grunting and making loud sounds)* THIS TO YOUR TYRANNY.

LESLIE:   Say "I don't have to hate them. I don't have to hate them."

DOCTOR:   Say "I don't have to hate them, I don't have to hate them."

GEORGE: I don't have to hate Mom, I don't have to hate Sally, I don't have to hate women, and *(with surprise)* I don't have to hate men, either.

DOCTOR: Say it again.

GEORGE: I don't have to hate women. I don't have to hate women. I don't have to hate women.

LESLIE *(low and serious):* I can love them. I can love them. I can love them.

GEORGE: I can love a woman. I can show her friendship *(voice beginning to rise)*. I can show my sister warmth. I can show her friendship. I CAN. I CAN. I CAN *(yelling)*. I CAN, I CAN, I CAN SHOW A WOMAN WARMTH, I CAN SHOW THEM FRIENDSHIP, I CAN SHOW THEM THEY ARE HUMAN BEINGS. I WILL, I WILL, I CAN, DO YOU UNDERSTAND? I CAN, I WILL *(breathing hard)*.

DOCTOR: What does your father say?

GEORGE: He can't say anything. He's gone.

DOCTOR: Do you want to say good-bye to him?

GEORGE *(pauses):* You're out of my life, Pop. YOU'RE OUT OF MY LIFE *(emphatically and with determination)*. *YOU'RE OUT OF MY LIFE.* I'll keep the strength I have. The weaknesses are gone. YOUR HATES ARE GONE *(speaking louder and faster)*. YOUR HATES ARE GONE *(yelling)*. YOUR HATES ARE GONE, GONE, GONE. THEY'RE GONE, THEY'RE GONE.

DOCTOR: Would you like to bury your father?

GEORGE *(hesitates, and then says):* Yes.

DOCTOR: Dig a hole in the floor, dig a grave in the floor, right there, then, and put him in it. (GEORGE *digs a grave in pantomime, breathing hard.)*

GEORGE *(picks his father up and lowers him gently into the grave):* OK, Pop, you're gone, you're gone.

DOCTOR: Put the earth back and stamp on it.

GEORGE *(does this, and then speaks in a breathless voice):* You're gone, you're gone *(stamping on the floor)*. Flatten out this mound. Flatten out this mound. No sign of it. No sign of it. No sign of it anymore.

DOCTOR: Do you feel better? [George *looks at me and nods—he is deeply stirred.*] Now, would you go—to the girls—that you hurt—and would you ask them if they will let you hold their hands, gently?

(GEORGE *goes to* VERA. *Their exchange has an air of quiet intimacy about it, warmth, gentleness, forgiveness—as do all of the following exchanges.*)

GEORGE   *(softly):* May I hold your hand?

VERA   *(softly):* Yes.

DOCTOR:   How's that, Vera?

VERA:   Very gentle.

GEORGE *(goes to* LAURA): Laura, will you let me hold your hand? (LAURA *nods and* GEORGE *holds her hand very gently).* I'm sorry for what happened.

LAURA   *(gently, almost inaudibly):* It's all right.

GEORGE:   Thank you.

DOCTOR:   How do you feel, Laura?

LAURA:   I feel good. A happy feeling . . .

DOCTOR:   Do you want to say anything else?

LAURA:   It's just a big change *(says this softly, and with a sense of wonder in her voice).*

(GEORGE *goes to* LINDA *and holds her hand gently).*

LINDA:   George, you said you want to be strong. You can be strong in a different way than you did earlier. (GEORGE *and* LINDA *look at each other.* GEORGE *lifts her hand and gently kisses it.*)

DOCTOR:   How do you feel, Linda, about George?

LINDA *(looking at* GEORGE): I feel—from your touch—that you're stronger and gentler, and that's good.

DOCTOR:   OK, will you look around, George, and see what you see?

GEORGE   *(full of emotion, surprise, incredulity):* I— never experienced a group of people in my life who looked so interested in me. I never experienced it in—in my whole life.

DOCTOR:   Will you look at the men—are you sure these men are your friends now?

GEORGE:   Yes, I am. And I feel I'm their friend.

DOCTOR:    How do you feel about the women?

GEORGE:    I feel good about the women *(half smiling, laughing),* I feel they're real live human beings.

LAURA:    It's just unbelievable watching you. It's just so beautiful. You've really made it beautiful.... What would you like to do? What would you like now?

GEORGE:    I'd sort of like to cry. I just want to be aware that you're a real live human being. (GEORGE *reaches over and touches* LAURA'S *hand.)* I just want to be aware that women are real live human beings, real live human beings. I'd like to be aware that I'm a real live human being.

DOCTOR:    I feel good about what you are doing, George.

TED:    I feel you're a real live human being.

LAURA:    I do too.

LINDA *(softly):* I do too.

DOCTOR:    Do you feel finished? Do you feel finished with this? (GEORGE *quietly and seriously nods his assent.)* Does anyone have any comments he wants to make?

MARK:    It isn't too late to do the things you want to do. You can change.

TED:    What could have been can still be.

MARK:    It just isn't too late, that's all.

# CHAPTER
# 7

*Naomi*

If ever I had a client who put the effectiveness of Transactional Analysis, Gestalt Therapy and nonverbal communication methods to the ultimate test as a useful therapeutic triumverate, it was Naomi Koslin.

Naomi came to see me on September 2, 1972, bitter, disillusioned, and angry. I saw her individually, and during the first session she told me about her background.

I learned that Naomi had lived in Antwerp with her mother, father, and brother when the Nazis were coming into power and during World War II.

As a child she received an indirect "Don't be you" injunction from her father, a Jew living in a Catholic community, who had denied his Jewishness to himself and his family, even before the development of anti-Semitic persecution by the Nazis. Hence he had denied to Naomi a part of her own inheritance. Even from the beginning she felt like an outsider in her community because her father's denial of his Jewishness to himself did not prevent others from knowing that he was, in fact, a Jew; and that Naomi too was a Jew, and hence different from them.

As anti-Semitic sentiment increased, Naomi received

from the community, the society, and the culture almost every injunction that children (who get them) usually receive from their parents. She definitely received the following:

1. Don't exist.
2. Don't be you.
3. Don't be a child.
4. Don't trust.
5. Don't make it.
6. Don't think.
7. Don't be important.
8. Don't show your feelings.
9. Don't have your feelings, you aren't entitled to them.
10. Don't enjoy.
11. Don't be sane.
12. Just plain *don't*.

These injunctions were given with the power of death behind them, and in fact, during the war, Naomi's mother, brother, and father were caught and murdered by the Gestapo.

You may wonder why I have selected the case of a person so remote from your personal experience as an example to illustrate the effectiveness of TA, Gestalt, and nonverbal communication methods in producing deep personality change. You may ask yourself: "What has the Jewish victim of a Nazi culture to do with my working out of my own problems? I, personally, have never faced anything so terrible in my own life." But the fact is that some children who are unloved by their parents and who received from them powerful and devastating injunctions actually do come to feel as if they were confined by harsh authorities in a concentration camp, or that they must flee these authorities—psychologically and emotionally—in order to survive.

The fact that Naomi received these injunctions from the

culture rather than from her parents turned out not to make any difference in the effectiveness of TA/Gestalt/nonverbal methods in producing a cure. As you will see, Naomi's problems of distrust, identity confusion, cynicism, fear of intimacy, and a hostile view of the world are, despite their origins, not so different from those felt by many people in contemporary American culture. The fact that she could change in response to therapy, after the extremities of her childhood and adolescence, shows the possibilities inherent in the procedures I am sharing with you—and, of course, is a telling example that you *can* change if you want to.

Now let's return to Naomi.

Although, even as a little girl, Naomi felt ostracized by her schoolmates, she was deeply loved by her family. In her own home, she was the pet, the little princess. Her mother's love and tenderness proved to be a crucial factor in Naomi's ability to survive increasingly difficult ordeals.

An incident that occurred when she was in the second grade stood out in her mind. One morning the school nurse, who knew Naomi was a Jew, came up to her and said, "You've got lice in your hair."

So far as Naomi knew, she certainly did not have lice in her hair, and her mother verified this later.

When Naomi got to class, the teacher stood up and said, "Who has lice in their hair?"

Some pupils raised their hands. Naomi didn't. Then the teacher, who also knew that Naomi was Jewish, said, "And you, Naomi?"

For some reason Naomi felt compelled to say, "Yes, me too."

Then the teacher said, "Not only do you have lice, but you lie on top of it. Get out of this class and go to the next class and tell the teacher that I'm sending you because I don't want you here. You're a liar."

The teacher in the next class said, "What's the matter?" Naomi had to tell her what had happened. The teacher said, very quietly, "You go and sit down—take an empty seat."

"The next day," Naomi told me, "my best friend, Gertrude, came to school. She had tears in her eyes. She looked at me and said, 'I can't play with you anymore.' I said, 'Why?' She said, 'My mother claims it's because of you that I have lice in my hair, so I can't play with you anymore.'. . . And that was the end of my friendship with Gertrude."

In describing to me her feelings about this, Naomi said, "When that happened I couldn't say a word. I guess I was learning to keep a façade." As it turned out, this capacity to hide her real feelings, which began with incidents like this, was one of the things that, in the end, saved Naomi's life.

A few months later, Naomi's father received an official letter from the Nazi Party telling him to report to Milan with his family on a certain day. "In other words," Naomi said, "we were set to go for deportation. My father knew what it was all about, but there was no way out. There was nowhere to go." As she said this, her voice was sad and lifeless.

The next day her father happened to meet Clara, a non-Jewish neighbor, on the street and said, "I want to say good-bye because tomorrow the four of us are going to Milan. We have been told to report there with the other Jews."

Clara became very angry and said, "We have a two-family house [she and her husband, Hans]. My father lives in the apartment upstairs. I'll speak to him and ask him if he will move downstairs. If he will, you can come into hiding with us and live in that apartment."

The following day Clara said to Naomi's father, "Never mind about going to Milan. Come into hiding with us."

It was in this casual, accidental way that Naomi's family found a place to hide. This is how close Naomi came to extermination in those early days of persecution.

For six months Naomi, who was then eight years old, her father and mother and her older brother, Joseph, together with Peter, Clara's oldest son, remained in that attic apartment. Peter, who was in his twenties, had been working for the underground and had been discovered; he was also in hiding.

Naomi said that going into hiding was not difficult for her at first. She felt it as a refuge from the increasing number of rejections, degradations, and insults she had been experiencing in the outside world.

One day, after Naomi and the others had been hiding for about six months, the Gestapo found out where they were. They pounded on the front door—a group of six men in Gestapo uniforms. Clara let them in. Naomi could hear them yelling, screaming and stomping, as they searched the first floor.

Then Naomi heard them coming up the stairs. She and the others were hiding in a third-floor closet, the door of which was covered with wallpaper to match the wallpaper on the walls, so that the door was invisible to the casual glance, though it could be discovered by minute inspection.

The Gestapo went through the second floor systematically. Then they came up to the attic. Naomi remembers the rough sounds of their feet on the attic stairs.

They turned over tables, ransacked closets, yelled at Clara and threatened her, but they didn't discover the wallpapered door behind which Naomi and the four others hid silently, fearing for their lives.

Finally the Gestapo left.

A short while after this happened, Naomi's father and brother said they couldn't take it anymore. One morning, just before dawn, they left for Switzerland. Later, through the underground, Naomi heard that they had been picked up at the Swiss border by German soldiers. Her father was sent to Paris, where he was reported dying of a resurgence of malaria that he had caught as a young man in Africa. Her brother, Joseph, was deported. As Naomi told me this, she began to cry.

Clearly, the little attic apartment was no longer a safe

hiding place. Clara and Naomi's mother decided that the safest thing to do with Naomi would be to send her to a convent. Clara made the contacts.

The mother superior and directress of the convent said that she would take Naomi under one condition: that she convert to Catholicism. They would instruct her in Catholicism, baptize her, and give her a new name, a false name, for her own protection and the protection of the convent.

Naomi's mother agreed.

Naomi's new name was Mary Catherine Jessen. As Naomi recounted this to me, she said, "By this time there was already a numbness over me. The reality was that it was safer to hide me by changing my name, but I was beginning to lose track of my own identity.

"While I was in hiding in the attic," Naomi said, "I felt safe from all the things I had struggled against and that I couldn't change and couldn't accept at the same time, so it was a little difficult to leave this and enter the convent.

"Nevertheless, I befriended one girl there—Angela. Of course, Angela didn't know a *thing (voice lowered)* about my being Jewish. Nobody knew except three people—the head of the convent and two assistants. Angela and I got on relatively well.

"One day the head of the convent, a Polish nun, called me into her office and said, 'Your mother was picked up by the Gestapo.' She and her two assistants were standing, and so was I. They didn't approach me, and I didn't approach them. I was stunned. Nobody showed any feelings. It was as if she had said, 'Tomorrow you will switch classes.'

"I went outside and walked around in the garden for a while. Then I went to one of the three nuns, the one I was closest to, and said, 'May I please go to my room. I *must* be alone *(voice choking).*' She said, 'We cannot afford to jeopardize the convent. You must go on exactly as if nothing happened.' So I went to my next class.

"After class I sat staring toward the wall. Angela, my friend, came over to me and said, 'What's the matter?' I said, 'Nothing.' She said, 'Oh, come on, something is the matter. We're friends—you can tell me.' I told her what happened and that I was a Jew. Angela backed away as if she had *(long sigh)* never seen anyone like me. *'A JEW!'* she said, with vehemence. *The horror in her eyes!* I don't think I can ever forget it.

"It didn't take me two minutes to realize what I had done. So I went to the nun I had spoken to previously and said, 'Angela knows.' She said, 'Oh, my God.' Angela was at a very impressionable age and very fearful. The Catholic religion is that kind of religion—it makes use of fear. The nun called Angela in at once and made her swear on the Bible never to divulge what I told her. And Angela swore and stuck to her guns. After that we never spoke again, or, let's put it this way, Angela never spoke to me again.

"I had a difficult time sticking it out to the end of the war, but I did. In the meantime, I was instructed in the Catholic religion by a young Jesuit priest who taught theology. I put my heart and soul into learning. First of all, I had never had a religion because of my father's attitude. This was a religion that I had wanted since I was that high, because I wanted to be like everybody else. It was an identification for me, because Jesus was a Jew; that was important, and also I desperately needed something to hold on to. I absorbed that religion like wildfire. The priest told me that I was the only one in his classes in all his sixteen years of teaching that got a hundred, verbatim, on all his questions. And he knew I was a Jew.

"I became—I would say—a good Catholic."

After the war, Naomi left the convent, in which she had finished high school. She went to a Jewish agency and applied for a grant of money to go to college and finish her education. She was told that she was entitled to aid as a Jew, and that she could have it on the condition that she give up the Catholic religion and become a Jew again. "We're helping Jews, that's it," was the message.

Naomi had gone to a Jewish agency to seek aid in the first

place because these agencies have lists of who came back from the concentration camps—the survivors. "Ah—there was nobody there from my family," she said. Her voice was resigned.

"I wasn't willing to give up the Catholic religion, so I applied to a Catholic agency in Belgium and got a scholarship at one of the Catholic universities, where I finished my college education. Then I went to nursing school and finished that, too.

"I think the thing that I regret the most is that when I went to that university I kept the name of Mary Catherine Jessen. I divorced myself completely from my real name, Naomi Koslin. I rejected Naomi Koslin and I identified with Mary Catherine Jessen. I had suffered so much pain under the name of Naomi Koslin; my life had depended for so long on being known as Mary Jessen. I was confused. I had rejected Naomi Koslin, and yet, somehow, I felt I was more than just Mary Catherine Jessen. Who was I? I really didn't know."

It was in that state of mind that Naomi came to the United States and then sought my professional help.

In the first session it became clear that Naomi was a very sensitive, intelligent human being who had been through a harrowing experience that lasted for years and that had radically altered her personality. She obviously had a strong sense of survival and a will to live.

She was struggling against the conviction that people were out to get her. One might think that she would see her coming to America as a new beginning, having put the past behind her. However, even in this "land of freedom and opportunity" she was unable to shake off the destructive effect of her experiences with the Nazis. She was wary and defensive. There was a real split in her personality, which might well be called the "two faces of Naomi," but the split was clearly not indicative of schizophrenia, since there was no thought disorder.

In her work as a nurse, Naomi had understandable

difficulties with authority figures. She was unable to make close friendships. She had survived, but without warmth or trust.

Naomi's safety in the past had required that she not be her real self, and that she be extremely selective of the people she trusted. She felt that for the most part, whenever she had reached out to trust in the past she had been betrayed: her best friends had betrayed her, the German society had betrayed her, she had received no comfort at the convent when she was informed that her mother had been picked up by the Gestapo. The Jewish agency where she applied for help after the war had discounted her loyalty to the Church that had been responsible for saving her life.

The only persons who had not betrayed her were Clara and her husband and sons, Clara's father, and Naomi's own family. In spite of the fact that all the other members of her family were eventually caught by the Gestapo, they did not divulge Naomi's hiding place, even though the Gestapo routinely tried to get such information from captives.

Although Clara's family and her own kin had risked their lives to save her, Naomi, when she first came to see me, was too bitter to recognize their sacrifices.

As Naomi told me her story, her face was a mask. She allowed no feelings to show. She said her arms and legs felt numb and cold—psychosomatic evidence of extreme anxiety.

After seeing Naomi twice a week in private sessions for a month, I placed her in a group which met once a week for two and a half hours, and once a month for a twelve-hour marathon.

On September 30, 1972, Naomi attended her first marathon. There were eighteen men and women in the marathon, ten of whom were from Naomi's own group. All of the marathon members had been in therapy for a considerably longer time than Naomi, and they had developed feelings of warmth and trust toward each other.

In spite of the fact that the group members accepted her

and, to the extent to which this is possible on short acquaintance, trusted her, Naomi found that she could not accept them as *real,* nor could she trust them.

An excerpt of the tape transcript of this first marathon will give you a verbatim account of Naomi's reaction to the group.

I began the marathon by asking each person to tell his or her name. We then divided into pairs in which each person told his partner three things he wanted the other to know about him.

Following this exercise I began to secure contracts by asking each person how he wanted to be different at the end of the marathon.

When I came to Naomi I said, "Naomi, you're next. How do you want to be different?"

NAOMI:    I think I would like the rest of the day to feel, rather than trying to convince myself, that this group is real. ... Real people in a real setting. From my past experience it doesn't seem real. It seems as if we're all playing a game, as compared to the groups I have known while growing up. They didn't seem as willing to help one another and they certainly didn't seem interested in growth, their own or anyone else's. So I would like to erase, to a certain extent, the groups of the past.

As I say this, I keep on saying to myself over and over again, "Is this group I'm sitting in right now real? It has to be real, it must be real, it will be real." And through the reality of this kind of setting I want to find an identity. That's the feeling I would like to get to.

DOCTOR:    You would like to be convinced that the group is a real group, that the people are real.

NAOMI:    Yes. I would like to come out tonight, when I go home by myself in the car. I would like to have the feeling for once—an emotional feeling, that this is a good group, real, within this setting as well as outside of it; that this is an honest part of society that is interested in positive growth rather than in destruction. I can't quite believe that this is true, that it's a segment, you know, of a whole. That's probably why I attack the group members a little more brutally than I intend to, because I feel like piercing the nonauthentic—or so far as I know—the nonauthentic feeling of well-being which so many of you seem to have.

DOCTOR: Is it possible that feeling well seems strange to *you,* and, therefore, it doesn't seem authentic?

NAOMI: Feeling well individually is not strange to me. Within a group setting it is strange to me, yes.

DOCTOR: So, what you want to do is break down your old associations that groups are destructive.

NAOMI: Right, right. I *must* as a matter of fact, I must erase that *completely,* intellectually and emotionally, and then . . . not *try* to convince myself, but believe truly that my old convictions aren't the right ones. They *were* the right ones. You see, that's where my trouble lies. My old convictions *were* the right ones at the time. What is the truth now?

DOCTOR: What were the old convictions?

NAOMI: I would say my old convictions were that groups were destructive.

DOCTOR: Nazi groups? Is that what you are talking about?

NAOMI: Ah—during the war, the Nazis—it was all ganging up, grouping, identifying . . . you were placed in a certain category and then you were—

DOCTOR: What category were you placed in?

NAOMI: First of all, I was placed in a category where . . . you weren't allowed to have a personal identity.

DOCTOR: What was it?

NAOMI: Well, you are a Jew, and you are a *dirty* Jew. So right away you are identified with that group.

DOCTOR: Where was this?

NAOMI: In Belgium during the Nazi occupation. And as a Jew, you cannot go home. And so you have no identity. And this is real, it is not make believe.

DOCTOR: So you certainly were in a very dangerous

position, being a Jew in a Nazi-occupied country.

NAOMI:    Yes. The danger came when the war came.

DOCTOR:    So we have to say that what you are saying is true for the way it used to be. What you need to find out now is whether all groups in the present are like the groups you knew during the war. We have to find out whether it is true for this group, today. Are you justified in feeling frightened now?

NAOMI *(pause):*    I don't know if I would use the word "frightened." There is a certain element of fear in it, I admit it. I'm cynical more than frightened, and I would like to get away from the feeling of being that cynical.

DOCTOR:    Do you have any idea of how you might be able to do that in this group?

NAOMI *(speaking to group as a whole):* Perseverance—that's the only word that comes to my mind.

DOCTOR *(speaking to group as a whole):* The problem is that Naomi doesn't believe that this group is real, or that it's a good group, or whatever. So the thing is that her vision of this group is colored by her earlier experiences with the Nazis. The problem now for you, Naomi, is to distinguish whether the members of this group behave like Nazis. This requires discrimination on your part. I wonder if you would be willing to take a risk and try something.

NAOMI:    All right.

DOCTOR:    Would you go to five people in the group, any five you want, and will you try to find out if they are real? That is, if they are in fact what they appear to be on the surface.

NAOMI:    I should go to them?

DOCTOR:    Yes, go to them, touch them, ask whatever you want to ask, or hold their hands, or get near them. Find out if they are really real or not.

NAOMI *(goes to* LARRY): Larry, are you real?

LARRY:    I think so . . . yes.

DOCTOR:    How can you find out if Larry is real?

NAOMI *(her voice trembling):* Will you be honest with me as to what you see, be it positive, be it negative? . . . Will you base it on what you see and what you hear?

LARRY: Yes.... Right now I see ... ah ... a very, very honest person who is being very realistic. I think you want to make sure of what you're involved with. So to me that's very real.

(NAOMI *continues to make personal contact with four other members of the group.*)

DOCTOR: Now that you've been around to five people, how do you feel?

NAOMI: I've gotten some ... I think I let my senses work rather than my mind.

DOCTOR: Is that good?

NAOMI: Yes. From some I get a feeling of either honesty—or of wanting to be extremely honest. From some I didn't get that feeling.

DOCTOR: Are you any closer to feeling this group is real?

NAOMI: I don't think I'm any closer to feeling it's real. I'm closer to *wanting* to feel it's real.

DOCTOR: OK. Are you willing to let it go with that for now?

NAOMI: Yes.

The marathon had more of an impact on Naomi than she was aware of at the time. For the following week, she trusted the group enough to share with them the whole grueling story of what it was like to survive as a Jew during the Nazi occupation, some details of which I have already recounted in giving you Naomi's background. All of the group members were deeply touched and expressed their feelings of warmth, empathy, and admiration to Naomi for her ability to survive.

When the group met for its next session on October 10, Naomi made a surprising announcement. The following is a verbatim transcript of excerpts from the tape:

NAOMI: Now I decided last week—I decided after the

group—that I must pick myself up and go back to Antwerp. *I dread it.* But *I'm going (voice determined).* I'll fly to Luxemburg, and go to Antwerp the next day. Of course, I'm going back to the place where I last lived, and to the house where we were in hiding. I don't know whether the people are living there anymore, but, nevertheless, the place is there. And I'm going to the convent. I also—luckily enough my grandfather survived through the war. He died at the ripe old age of ninety-two in a Catholic nursing home. I'm not too sure where it was, but I will find it, and I will visit his grave, because—you know—I want to see *one grave (sense of determination and pride)* with the name of Koslin on it. And I want to identify— *(Her voice is choked with emotion. There is a long pause.)*

DOCTOR:   How do you feel about going?

NAOMI:   I dread it. I begin to regret it, but I *must go.* I must see if I can get something back. I haven't got the faintest idea. But I think there must be something.

DOCTOR:   Do you think you might be able to contact the little girl?

NAOMI:   Who? Angela?

DOCTOR:   Naomi.

NAOMI *(in an anguished voice):* Me—that's what I'm hoping for. Yes—ah—oh—that's what I want. I'm hoping to. Sometimes I feel that I died there. I'm lost as to who I am.

DOCTOR:   So maybe you can go back to find out who you are and start over again. I think it's very crucial that you go back because I'm sure that all of the fantasy and thinking you've done about it—

NAOMI:   I would prefer the word "deburden" to fantasy. I don't consider this a fantasy—I consider this a great big burden.

DOCTOR:   I agree with you.

NAOMI:   I've been thinking of some of the positive things that happened before the war. I remember very warmly when I got a new coat, and my mother and I were walking arm in arm to the store to buy a matching scarf.

And a silly little ice skate pin which I adored—a pin—which was the only thing I brought to the States, that I salvaged. . . . I remember I was feeling very good that day—I went to an ice cream parlor with her and kind of stuck myself up with some gooey kind of sundae. Some day, I intend to do that, of course. And I'll go to the place where my father used to hang out with his cronies . . . and the times he took me. I intend to go back and—

DOCTOR: Back to some of the old places before the war?

NAOMI: Right. I feel a little bad that I am going with such pressure in me.

DOCTOR: When did the pressure to go back build up?

NAOMI: After the marathon. When I thought about what you said, you know. A couple of key questions you asked me about why I didn't accept the pleasant experiences with the other people. I didn't trust the people in the marathon as being honest when they treated me well. Any experience—good, bad, or indifferent—it didn't seem as if anything was being absorbed. And I felt that most of me was back over there, left behind, and I decided to go back and see whether that's not so. I don't know. I just felt a tremendous urge. I felt, let me do it now. I wish I didn't have to do it alone, but there is no way that I could do it with anyone else.

DOCTOR: If you would, go out on the streets and experience that you can safely go out on the streets in that same place; because if you had gone out on the streets before you would have been picked up and killed. Now you can go on the streets and not be picked up. You'll be safe. It's important to get that deeply into you. Otherwise, the memory remains indelible. It's very good to go back and see it as it is now, which is very different than what it was. I think it all relates to what you said at the marathon, which is that it's all very well to have nice experiences with so-called nice people, but you couldn't trust anyone, and so you couldn't really experience, couldn't feel that it could be for real. And I can understand the feeling, and sympathize with it. It's really important to try to do something to get out of that.

NAOMI: That's number one. And also I feel part of me is really dead, has died, over there *(speaking very fast, and under intense pressure)*. I don't know what to do with that either.

DOCTOR: Go over and experience it as deeply as you can. Get into all the experiences as deeply as you can. Let your feelings come back again, so that you experience yourself again.

NAOMI: Once I'm there I can assure you ... that's one place that I know ... that I will *have* to feel ... I have no choice.

GROUP MEMBER: I wonder if part of it is that you feel guilty being alive when so many people who were over there are dead. Is that why you are calling yourself dead?

NAOMI: Well, I think—ah—but this is something I acknowledged a long time ago. Of course there is a guilt. That's an irrational guilt, and there is nothing I can do about it. The irrational guilt is I survived, they died, of course. That I've known all along and have accepted that. But my thought about that is the experience of the adult. I must go back to the feelings that I experienced growing up. Now my experiences have been toward destruction, with the exception of my own family. They have been always toward destruction, and never toward life. In other words, I should have been dead. [*The "Don't exist" message.*] Not just the physical death, but every other way of dying. The forces outside of my family were always geared to destruction. I would say a part of me—I don't know how much of me—but a great big good part has been destroyed. I feel angry about that. And bitter.

DOCTOR: It's true that an important segment of the population that was in control was bent on killing you. However, there were others who were bent on saving you, and I would like to hear something about them. I haven't heard much about them. They risked their lives, for whatever reasons they did it—maybe it was for money, maybe it was for you, maybe—

NAOMI: Are you talking about the people who were hiding us?

DOCTOR: Yes.

NAOMI: No, that wasn't for money. That was strictly a humanitarian—strictly very much that.

DOCTOR: So I would like you to think who was it that risked their lives for you. It isn't that all people were out to get you. Some were out to get you. But some people were out to save you, and I would like you to get in contact with that, if you will. Who were the people who saved you, when you went in hiding, without whom you would have been caught?

NAOMI: You mean the family where we went in hiding—the first family that took us in. You want me to talk about them, is that it?

DOCTOR: Yes.

NAOMI: There was the husband, Hans, and wife, Clara, and the two younger brothers. And also Peter, in the underground.

DOCTOR: Who would have been killed if you had been discovered.

NAOMI: If we had been discovered.

DOCTOR: So in fantasy will you put them on this chair and talk to them. [*Double-chair technique.*]

NAOMI *(long pause):* I remember you very clearly. I think I remember you better than I remember anything else. *(Turning to* DOCTOR.*)* I remember the husband—I think they were Scandinavian—I remember him as a pleasant, jolly, tall built man. I remember his wife as a warm, nice-looking, friendly woman. The middle son was maybe two years older than I was. I see him a well brought up nice boy, and I remember the youngest was very playful, a little bored, not very much concerned with what was going on in the house. He was about seven or eight.

DOCTOR:    Did he know about you?

NAOMI:    He knew we were there.

DOCTOR:    And he was out in the community with the Nazis.

NAOMI:    Yes.

DOCTOR:    And he heard them talking about the Jews?

NAOMI:    Yes—yes.

DOCTOR:    And he didn't say anything?

NAOMI:    He didn't say anything.

DOCTOR:    Will you put him on the chair and talk to him?

NAOMI *(long pause):*    I don't know what your parents told you. *(Speaking to* DOCTOR.*)* I have a feeling that he didn't know exactly who we were—but he knew that his parents rented the room upstairs to people who never went out.

DOCTOR:    But he didn't talk about that, or that would have been the end.

NAOMI:    No, he didn't talk.

DOCTOR:    So his parents must have told him something, so that he didn't talk.

NAOMI:    I don't know what they told him—I don't know.

DOCTOR:    It's really amazing, though. He was so young, and everybody's life depended on what he was saying.

NAOMI:    Yes, I—

DOCTOR:    So, how do you feel about that?

NAOMI:    Somehow I'm more impressed with the middle one. I always saw the younger one as a little playful boy who wasn't very much concerned with what was going on upstairs. I have a much more vivid impression of his brother. He knew definitely what was going on, and was going to school *(long pause)*. I think I'm very much impressed with his humanity. [*This is the first expression of any kind of appreciation on* NAOMI'S *part. She voluntarily puts him on the chair and speaks to him.*] I am impressed with the fact that you must have known what the penalty was. The fact that you had strangers in your house may have cost your parents' life, your life. I don't quite understand what your parents taught you. I don't know how you were brought up. I feel awfully sorry that I didn't have a chance to get to know you much, much better. I would have liked the chance very, very much. I would like to have talked to you more. To have been much closer to you *(long pause)*. I feel the same way about your mother.

DOCTOR: Put her on the chair and talk to her. What was her name?

NAOMI: Clara *(pause)*.

DOCTOR: Just talk to her.

NAOMI: It's funny, the thought went through my head that they were Catholic, but they were Protestant.

DOCTOR: Tell her how you feel about her keeping you.

NAOMI *(long pause):* You are one of the nicest, warmest adults that I've ever known, that I have—I know—I wish I was able to *(voice breaking)* to—to express to you *(tears in her voice)* the feelings—of—humanity that you have given me. I think from you came out—a—a—human experience which is—which was far beyond any human relationship that I have ever experienced since *(long pause)*. I think—you just as much as my parents—have *given me the will to live (twenty-second pause). (To* DOCTOR.) I feel the same way about—I remember her husband very vividly.

DOCTOR: What do you remember? Talk to him.

NAOMI *(long sigh):* You were—I remember your being very gay. I remember your treating me like a little girl—you were very tall and I was very little—you kind of—got a kick out of me—hugging me—telling me not to worry. Telling me that—should there come a time when my parents could not afford to buy on the black market anymore, that there was nothing to worry about, because as long as you had, I would have, or we would have. Dick, I'm feeling something right now. Is it all right if I tell you how I feel right now? *(Long pause.) I feel this—I think I'm amazed at the warmth that I feel right now.* I feel very, very much alive in this particular moment in a very positive way. I almost feel—and this is a total reversal from when I came in tonight—I almost feel as if I can't *wait* to get to Antwerp on Thursday and stand in front of their little house.

DOCTOR: And what will you think when you are standing in front of it?

NAOMI: I think I am going to sit on the doorstep and I am going to just *cry (emphasis on cry, as if that is a thing that she has been wanting to do for a long time).*

DOCTOR: I'll be thinking of you. And what will your tears say?

NAOMI: They will say, "Thank you" *(crying).* For showing a bit of humanity. Oh—ah—all that goddamned destruction and filth *(voice breaking).* Not a little bit of humanity, a *lot* of humanity. Say thank you for being able to feel more now.

DOCTOR: Is there any chance that you could contact any of them? *(Voice warm and sympathetic.)*

NAOMI: I hope so. I—I—don't know. This was a long time ago. I am going to go to the town magistrate. I am going to try very hard to see if there is anyone that knew them *(pause).* If I can't find them—I'll make sure—within me—that they get—that they get their thanks—within me. Again, it will be a present from them to me. But I'll make sure that I remember very, very clearly and very surely.

DOCTOR: Will you let this feeling be in you and "own" it? This feeling of your humanity and their willingness to sacrifice for their beliefs? And will you let it oppose the destructive things that happened? [*Permission.*] And be with you to help you be on the positive side?

NAOMI: Yes *(said with a soft, religious feeling).*

DOCTOR: I would like you to have a little conversation if you will, playing the part of you that says, "Everything is evil, and I can't trust," with—the mother.

NAOMI: With whom?

DOCTOR: With the mother of that family that saved you.

NAOMI: All right. [*In this double-chair gestalt,* NAOMI *starts as not trusting.*] *(To Clara.)* I'm sorry, I don't trust anyone. I don't trust anyone—I don't want to be close to anyone. I'm willing to be civilized, but I don't want to pay more than that.

DOCTOR: Now change chairs, be the mother, and talk back to you.

NAOMI: Naomi, you don't mean that. You can't mean that. You mean that what we did counted so little?

DOCTOR: Be Naomi now.

NAOMI *(long pause):* I'm going to give you—I'm willing to return to you—I'm willing to accept—what you have given me. I'm willing to build on it. I'm willing to grow on it.

DOCTOR: Be Clara now.

NAOMI *(hesitating, uncertain).*

DOCTOR *(speaking to Clara):* Would you like Naomi to build on what you did?

NAOMI *(long pause):* This was our aim, Naomi, to let you live. We want you to live as much as our own children. We took the risk with our children for your life. You *must* build on it.

DOCTOR: Be Naomi and talk back.

NAOMI: I understand you. I understand you fully. But why must I build—why must I build—on your humanity? Why must I build on the chance you took? Wasn't there room for my own humanity?

DOCTOR: You tell her why you need to build on it. Tell her what it did for you.

NAOMI: I don't think I feel anger coming into me. I feel like—I feel resentment that she had to give me—all that much—at such a tremendous price—for what? Why? For what? What did she have to take a chance for? Why? *(There is anguish in her voice.)*

DOCTOR: Be Clara now. (NAOMI *doesn't respond.*) Be her now. Tell Naomi why you took a chance.

NAOMI *(twenty-second pause)* (NAOMI *as Clara*): I took a chance because I saw you in danger—I saw human lives—and I wasn't one of them either. My father would apologize for them—and I apologize by offering my life *(sudden catch in* Naomi's *voice)* and my home for you. I don't know how well I can express—this is my apology—my giving. I feel I've given all.

Doctor: Be Naomi. How does her giving that make you feel? Tell her how you feel.

Naomi *(long pause):* I feel both anger and tremendous gratitude and warmth toward you. That society has placed on you and me that kind of predicament, where we had to—at such a cost—at such a price—I love you and I thank you. For showing that piece of humanity.

Doctor: Will you tell her if you want to be on the side of humanity yourself?

Naomi: I don't know if I want to be. I really don't know—

Doctor: Tell Clara how you feel.

Naomi: I don't know what I feel like. I don't know. I think I've got so much anger and frustration left in me that I don't know. If I could be where you were, Clara—in all truthfulness, the way you are—I would want to be where you are.

Doctor: Say that again.

Naomi: If I could really be in all honesty where you are, as you are, oh, God yes, I would want to be.

Doctor: Will you say, "I can be where you are"?

Naomi: I can be?

Doctor: Yes, "I can be where you are, if I choose to. I have the power to be where I want to be. I can be where you are." Will you say that?

Naomi: No, I won't say that.

Doctor: What will you say?

Naomi *(long pause):* I cannot be where you are.

Doctor: What would you like to say to her now?

Naomi: I would like to be where you are, but I can't be where you are *(voice resigned).* I cannot be where you are, because if I want to visit the graves of my parents, I must go to Buchenwald, and Auschwitz, and Dachau *(voice rising and angry).* You can simply go to a graveyard *(crying).* I can't be where you are. I wish I could *(longing in* Naomi's *voice, and pathos; long pause).*

DOCTOR: Will you put your own mother on the chair now? Would you do that?

NAOMI: Yes.

DOCTOR: Can you see her?

NAOMI: Yes, I can.

DOCTOR: Will you say whatever you would like to say to her?

NAOMI: Mom—you were a great gal—you really were. I always felt you should spank me a little more. I'm glad you didn't. I need your warmth. You were easy to manipulate, and I did. You were very accepting—and—you loved me an awful lot. I have no doubt about that. I've always needed you an awful lot. I think more so once I went out of the house than before that. I remember needing you much more desperately once I went to school. I needed you to warm up the home, your lap to climb on—uh—ah—

DOCTOR: Talk to your mother about the days you were in hiding with her. How was she to you?

NAOMI: Mom, you were the same as you always were—warm, loving, honest. She cared about me *(pause).* I feel very—I'm very grateful to you, yes, for being the kind of mother you've been all along.

DOCTOR *(voice warm and sympathetic):* Would you be your mother now and tell Naomi how you feel about her?

NAOMI *(pause):* Honey—you were my daughter—you were the youngest one, my little girl. I—would have given my life for you *(voice low and sweet).*

DOCTOR: Is Naomi very precious to you?

NAOMI *(playing role of her mother):* Yes, Naomi is extremely—you are extremely precious Naomi, *yes you are.*

DOCTOR: Be Naomi now and say how you feel about that.

NAOMI:    Mom—I've known that all along. I feel that I also know that that has kept me going. [*Here we see the positive scripting that made it possible for* NAOMI *to survive.*] The reason that I truly survived. It is the reason why I wanted to survive. I have something that you gave me—worthwhile having—you gave me freedom—ah—as a little kid, and it's that that I am convinced, and I know deep within me, that is what makes me sit here—that's what is part of why I want to live. [*Winner's Script.*] Somehow that personifies, I guess, the joy of living.

DOCTOR:    Will you say that again?

NAOMI:    Because to me that personifies that kind of joy of living.

DOCTOR:    Say it again.

NAOMI:    What you gave me—was joy of living.

DOCTOR:    Are you glad to have that?

NAOMI:    Oh, yes I—oh, yes I am. *Yes (said with definiteness and finality).*

DOCTOR:    Naomi, will you say good-bye to your mother now? Will you say what you would like to say to your mother and then say good-bye to her?

NAOMI:    Mom, you can take credit for my wanting to live. I don't mean JUST LIVE WITH A SMALL L, BUT LIVE WITH A CAPITAL L. Of course I'll never forget you, but I must say good-bye to you now. I'll remember you the way I remember you now. When I stand in front of our home, I will say good-bye to you, too *(long pause).*

DOCTOR:    This is it, Mom. I'm saying good-bye to you.

NAOMI *(softly and gently):*    Mom, I am saying good-bye to you.

DOCTOR:    Do you want to say anything else to her before you say good-bye?

NAOMI:    No, no.

DOCTOR:    How does she look as you say good-bye to her?

NAOMI:    As somebody who understands what I am

trying to say and what I am trying to do. Very much human.

DOCTOR:   How do you feel while you say good-bye to her?

NAOMI:   I feel very calm. I don't feel like a little girl at all. I feel warmth. *(Looking at* DOCTOR.) My arms and legs were cold when I came in. Now they are warm.

DOCTOR:   Will you tell your mother that your arms and legs were numb and cold, but now they are warm again?

NAOMI *(to mother):*   My arms and legs were numb and cold, but they are not now. They're *very* much alive, very, very warm. I love you, Mom. Good-bye *(softly and gently)*. I will always love you. I will always love you. I will say good-bye to you now.

DOCTOR:   Is she going away?

NAOMI:   Yes, I think she's going. I'm not so sure I want her to go. But she's going.

DOCTOR:   Do you want to call her back again?

NAOMI:   I want to give her something. I don't know what I want to give her.

DOCTOR:   What do you want to give her?

NAOMI:   Life. But I can't, can I, Mom? You're dead now.

DOCTOR:   "You're alive in me, Mom. There's a lot of good in me from you, Mom." Would you tell her that before she leaves?

NAOMI:   Mom, you left an awful lot in me. Your warmth is in me—it is there—I promise you, Mom, I will let it be. I'll let you live in me. I'm going to pray hard not to erase that.

DOCTOR:   Say it again.

NAOMI:   I'm going to try—uh—very, very hard not to erase that. I'm going to let you be.

DOCTOR:   "Let it grow in me."

NAOMI:   Yes, let it expand.

DOCTOR:   "Your love is still with me and it's still alive."

NAOMI:   Yes, your love for me, mine for you, is *there*.

DOCTOR   *(pause):* Feel finished now?

NAOMI:   Yes, I think I feel finished.

DOCTOR:   Want to say one last good-bye?

NAOMI:   No.

DOCTOR:   OK. *(Pause.)* How are you feeling now?

NAOMI:   I am so deeply into this that I don't know which is the real me.

DOCTOR:   Will you look around the room now, and see what you see? Make contact.

NAOMI *(long pause—she looks around):* It's—it's— (NAOMI'S *voice is choked and full of feeling. She is having difficulty talking.)*

DOCTOR:   What do you see?

NAOMI *(long pause):*   I see human beings.

DOCTOR:   Are they real?

NAOMI:   Yes, I think they're real *(voice choked, and talking with effort)*. I think they're real.

DOCTOR:   Would you go to each person and ask anything you want to?

NAOMI:   OK. *(Pause. Walking over to* JIM.) Will you be able to accept me as I am?

JIM *(looking at her closely and compassionately):*   Yes. (NAOMI *continues to go to other members of the group and make a direct contact. All of the members respond with concern and warmth. After* NAOMI *had gone to each person, I said:)*

DOCTOR:   How do you feel now?

NAOMI:   How do I feel now?

DOCTOR:   Yes.

NAOMI:   I feel an awful lot of the OK Child in me.

DOCTOR:   What does that feel like?

NAOMI:   It doesn't make sense. It feels like swing your arms and say "Yippee!"

DOCTOR:   Be a little girl. Swing your arms and say "Yippee!" *(Pause.)* Let it out. Come on.

NAOMI *(laughing, but not otherwise responding).*

DOCTOR: I'll do it with you. Or do you want to do it alone?

NAOMI: No, I don't want to do it alone.

JOYCE: We can all do it. Let's all do it!

DOCTOR: When I count three, let's all yell, "Yippee!" And you swing your arms, Naomi.

NAOMI *(laughing happily):* I'll swing my arms.

DOCTOR: One, two, three—

EVERYBODY: YIPPE-E-E!

OWEN: I think every night at nine twenty-five we should all stand up and yell, *"YIPPEE!"* I'm serious. Remember, *we're* with you over there.

NAOMI: I will. I really will.

DOCTOR: I have an impulse to rock you.

NAOMI *(surprised):* You want to rock me?

DOCTOR: Yes.

NAOMI: All right.

DOCTOR: I need several people. Stand in a circle close to Naomi. Now, Naomi, you lean back on my arms. Now everyone help lift Naomi up waist high, so someone is supporting her legs and thighs and buttocks and back and shoulders. Let her head hang down, don't touch it, so she can experience the rocking more freely.

(NAOMI *leans back and is picked up by me and the group members—ten persons.)*

DOCTOR: Don't talk; the experience will be deeper if you don't talk. Now rock Naomi back and forth. *(Group is rocking* NAOMI *back and forth.)* Now hum, *Om—*

*(Everyone hums with the rocking—*Om—*and it sounds like a big bumblebee, very reassuring.* NAOMI *has the faintest trace of a smile on her lips.)*

DOCTOR: Now lower her, ever so gently, to the floor. Naomi, you lie quietly with your eyes closed, and absorb the experience.

*(Thirty seconds of complete silence, while* NAOMI *is lying on her back on the floor with her eyes closed.)*

DOCTOR: Now everyone very gently stroke Naomi.

*(Everyone does this. Some stroking her hands and arms, some her legs, some her face.)* Now slowly open your eyes, Naomi. *(Pause.)*

(NAOMI *opens her eyes, looks at various members of the group.)*

DOCTOR:    How do you feel now, Naomi?

NAOMI *(quietly):*    I think I'll make it.

Naomi left for Antwerp the day after this session. The next week, when the group met, I said, "Naomi isn't here. She is in Antwerp, and we all know why. Let's have one minute of silence to think about Naomi, each in his own way."

The next group session that Naomi attended was on October 24, after her visit to the scenes of her childhood. I started the group by saying to Naomi, "We all want very much to know what happened to you in Antwerp."

The following excerpts are taken from a transcript of the tape I made of the October 24, 1972, session.

NAOMI:    I arrived Thursday night in Antwerp. . . . The next morning I went to the house where we had lived before the war and explained to the nice young woman who lived there why I wanted to see it. She let me in, and I went through some very deep feelings. *(Long pause.)*

After that I went to the superintendent of the school where Gertrude and I had gone before the war. She was the girl whose mother said I had given her lice and she couldn't play with me anymore. The superintendent had a very, very hard time tracing her; she had to call the official building. Well, the superintendent spent the whole afternoon with me, and finally I found Gertrude. She was living right across from the apartment where we used to live. . . . It was about six or seven o'clock when I got to Gertrude's house. She was very surprised to see me. . . . Her house was a very beautiful one. And I was very surprised to learn that she never married. I had thought of her as having four or five kids. We spent the evening together. And I *don't* know how to describe this feeling. We looked at each other a lot. We talked a lot with each other, you know—

DOCTOR: What were your feelings when you looked at her?

NAOMI: What were my feelings? I had a great deal of warmth for her. We had been very good friends before the war. She was the only good girl friend I can remember, and we had good feelings.

DOCTOR: You had good feelings when you looked at her.

NAOMI: Yes. And she had a very good feeling when she looked at me. I said, "Gertrude, do you remember why we stopped being friends?" And she said, "I'm not quite sure." I said, "Do you remember the story about the lice in my hair?" She said, "No, not exactly." I said, "Your mother blamed me for giving you lice." Gertrude said, "Well, there were only the two of us, so who else could it have been?" I said, "Gertrude, half the class had lice. Anyway, neither of us has lice now; we are both very well groomed. So let's forget about it." That broke the ice. She was really *very* happy to see me, and I was *very* happy to see her.

(NAOMI *goes on to explain how she finally located Clara, the woman who had hidden her and her family during the Nazi occupation. Clara had moved to the suburbs of Antwerp.*)

NAOMI: I walked in there, and of course I didn't realize that Clara is now seventy. And I walked in there and I looked at her and I recognized her, but she didn't recognize me. She said, "Yes?" I said, "I'm Naomi." And Clara's face . . . she couldn't believe it . . . and she took . . . she grabbed me and she pulled me into the hall of her house. And she said, "Wait for Hans, you must see Hans" *(her husband).* And when he came in he hugged me as if . . . he kind of squeezed me to death.

DOCTOR: How did you feel?

NAOMI: *I felt immense. (Great satisfaction in voice.)*

And I felt afterwards very, very grateful to you, Dick, for making me face them the night before I left. You made me talk to all these people. So I felt close to them all, and what we did in the gestalt became reality. And I felt *very, very good.* I learned something from Hans that I haven't quite digested yet. He said, "You know, we have brought Jews over from Holland, have smuggled diamonds for them, gold for them—you are the only one who came back." And then he said, "Thank you." (NAOMI'S *voice shows satisfaction.*)

The next morning Hans and I walked through a section of Antwerp that used to be a Jewish area. . . . Now there is only one Jewish family left . . . and I got a very eerie feeling, you know, walking into that Jewish area which is not Jewish anymore. I felt *very, very happy to be alive.* It was as if a feeling of real life surged through my whole body *(voice vibrant).* And I was extremely grateful to be alive.

A few days later I went back to the convent that had taken me in. And that had changed an awful lot. Very much modernized. It was like the Middle Ages when I was there. The nun who was the head of the convent when I was in hiding wasn't there, but the one who was second in command was there. And she couldn't believe her eyes when she saw me. I arrived there at eleven o'clock in the morning, expecting to be out by eleven fifteen. I didn't leave that place until five o'clock in the afternoon. We spent the whole afternoon together . . . everything and anything. That one favorite nun of mine had transferred to a convent in Milan, where we were to be deported. I called her. She was extremely happy to hear from me and said she thought of me many times.

Then I got the address of Angela, who had been my friend in the convent till she learned I was a Jew. I called her and she said, "I'll pick you up in the lobby of your hotel at nine tomorrow morning." I was sitting in the lobby at nine o'clock. Angela came. *(Satisfaction in voice.)* She hadn't changed much. Five children, five grown-up children! It was again as if nothing had happened. As if there never had been a war. We were like two students together in her home. That afternoon we took a walk in the beautiful countryside. As we were walking arm in arm, I said, "Angela, do you remember . . . why we did not stay friends?" And it's funny how people can tell themselves something and believe it. She said, "Yes, I've been thinking about it, sometimes. It's because we both were stubborn, wasn't it, and we didn't get along too well?" I said, "Angela, we never had a fight. You wouldn't speak to me anymore when you found out I was a Jew." *(Voice reproachful.)* Angela looked up at me and tears came into her eyes—and she hugged me. I said, "Well, I will tell you, maybe I didn't understand two weeks ago, or three weeks ago, but I understand now. I understand what your feelings were, I understand the responsibility it was for you. I *really* understand the way you were brought up, you know, with anti-Semitism; you didn't know what a Jew was all about." Angela says, "Really, did I really, really *(voice incredulous)* do that?" I said, "You really, really, really did that. That's what happened. . . ." We spent the whole day there with her husband and four of her children. It was a happy day. That night I left Angela and went back to my hotel.

The next day I just walked all over to the places which are of interest to me. I felt, as I walked, that I was beginning to find Naomi again. I began to want to come back to New York. The next day I caught the plane, very, very eagerly. I feel very different now than two weeks ago.

DOCTOR: How do you feel different now from the way you felt before you went to Antwerp?

NAOMI: A great deal of anger has evaporated—has gone away. I think that in Belgium my anger replaced itself with sadness, when I saw these sections, you know, where Jewish people lived—the section where we used to live, and all that. And then the sadness turned into a sudden feeling of wanting to be free of Antwerp and all the terrible things that happened there.

On the plane I had a thought. I said to myself, "You know what you should have done, Naomi? When you were buying your ticket in Antwerp back to New York, you should have put down your suitcase and screamed out loud, *'Good-bye, Antwerp, good-bye.'* " *(Voice loud and carefree.)* And that's the way I felt. I felt, "Good-bye, it was nice knowing you, I came back to you, to see those I wanted to see. Everyone received me warmly." And, as I said this to myself, I think my anger went with it, and then I got that *tremendous good feeling of going Home, capital "H,"* to the United States—home to my family, home to this group, and it became all one great big HOME. And with the realization of capital "H," I became very excited to be alive. And that's where I stand now.

DOCTOR: That's great. *(Group members start applauding loudly.)*

NAOMI: And of course I ask myself, "Now you are Home, capital H, where do you want to go? I think this is what I want. I have a lot of childness in me. I know. I'm totally aware of it. Not an Adapted Child, but an authentic Child. Given the opportunity I think I would like to let it out as much as I can.

DOCTOR: The Free Child.

NAOMI: The Free Child.

DOCTOR: You have a good one.

NAOMI: I don't know if it's a good one, but I have a lot of it. I would like very much to have that Free Child grow up into an uncontaminated adult. I think there I have a way to go. I don't know exactly how to go, but—ah—with advisement, directions, and what I can come up with within myself, I am very much willing to reach that goal. To be an authentic adult.

DOCTOR: That's beautifully said, in just the right way. It takes a period of growth to go through stages that you missed.

NAOMI: Yes.

DOCTOR: When you were in hiding.

NAOMI: Yes.

DOCTOR: And you can go through them right in this group.

NAOMI: Yes.

If this were a movie instead of real life, Naomi's return to Antwerp, and her happy feeling of "coming home" again to the United States, to her family, and to the group might well be the end of her story. But from the therapeutic standpoint it is only the beginning, for Naomi had not yet "come home" to herself.

Her personality was still fragmented, and she literally did not know who she was. She wanted to find a self, an identity. She wanted to be free, independent, and trusting. But her personality was split, and two separate parts of Naomi fought for survival and dominance. There was the Free Child—the little Jewish girl who was loved by her family, but who had to go into psychic as well as actual hiding; and there was the strong, cynical Adapted Child— the Catholic girl who survived, but with great bitterness. Each wanted to get rid of the other.

The following transcript dated January 9, 1973, describes how Naomi began to integrate her personality and to find her own identity.

NAOMI: I would like to work on something very specific tonight—I would like to work on being integrated. I still feel different parts within myself, from my background and upbringing. I have never been able to integrate them so that I felt like a total human being. Different pieces—I would like to bring them, you know, into one. I would like to feel myself, whatever that person will be. I would like to feel an "I." I feel now like several little complete people, but not one person. In one direction there is a person. In another direction there is another person. I would like to integrate, but I don't know how to do it.

DOCTOR: So let's start on it. Let's imagine that all

your dissociated elements are floating around in this room, and you reach out and grab one at a time and describe it, and then put it in you.

NAOMI: All right. Well, the first thing that is over-whelming is the Adapted Child. The moment the Free Child stepped out of the house and couldn't be a Free Child anymore, she had to become adapted. And that Adapted Child has grown and grown. She was very, very necessary, or I wouldn't have survived. . . . But she's a pain in the neck now. First, society wouldn't let her be a Free Child, so she had to become an Adapted Child out of necessity. Then, of course, the Adapted Child saved my life; then she grew so much that she began to eat me up alive. I don't want her anymore. She's of no use to me.

DOCTOR: Would you like to bury her?

NAOMI: Maybe I'm a little skeptical of burying her. I would just like to let go of her.

DOCTOR: All right. Well, let's work on that, then.

NAOMI: Mmmm. . . .

DOCTOR: Put your Adapted Child on this chair and you sit on this chair facing her. [*Double-chair gestalt.*] What ego state do you want to be in when confronting her?

NAOMI: I would like to be in the Free Child, but I sort of hesitate to do this because when I was in hiding, in misery, the Free Child that I developed during the first six years of my life got frightened and ran away. She became sort of manicky. So if I get in touch with her now, I'm afraid I might lose control and become manic.

DOCTOR: Get into your Adult first. Be in your Adult and talk to your Adapted Child.

NAOMI: All right, I am going to be in my Adult. . . . Well, Adapted Child—adapted Naomi—ah—you over-whelm me. I know intellectually that you're no good for me, that I don't need you, I don't want you. And yet you've played a very good service. You made it possible for me to survive. *(Pause.)* I—I—you've made me hide pain—you've made me put up a front, you've made me—my face, very often into a mask so people didn't even realize how they were hurting me. You made me look as if it didn't matter what happened when it did. I think it's about time that I let you go *(voice determined)* no matter *what.* I don't know what will appear, I don't know what will be, but I would like to let you go, because your function, really and truly, is finished.

DOCTOR:   Tell your Adapted Child why you don't want her right now.

NAOMI *(pause):*   I don't want you anymore because I don't need a façade anymore. I'm not in danger now. Nobody is trying to hurt me, to knife me; nobody's there to belittle me, nobody is there to step on me. Nobody is there to *kill* me. And you keep on ... hanging on to me, or I'm hanging on to you ... I don't know. It's very hard. You overwhelm me, really; you have really taken over, and I don't want it. I don't want it that way. I want to feel free and I want to come to the surface. *I want to own me ...* I want to get me back.

DOCTOR:   Now play the role of your Adapted Child. (NAOMI *moves to the other chair.)* What do you want for yourself, Adapted Child?

NAOMI [*as Adapted Child*]:   Why should you let me go? Look at all the things I've done for you. Look how much I've been hiding for you. I've made you look and act like an adult, instead of whining and crying and diminishing and shrinking. I've done a good job for you. Why would you let me go now? I demand to be here. I demand to continue ... I would like to be recognized.

DOCTOR:   What would you like to be ... what kind of things would you like to be recognized for ... what kind of response do you want?

NAOMI [*still in Adapted Child*]:   I've put up a front for you. And you accepted that front, out of necessity. I want acknowledgment.

DOCTOR:   OK, Adapted Child. Now be in your Adult.

NAOMI [*in Adult*]:   I acknowledge what you've done for me. I acknowledge.

DOCTOR: Do you like what your Adapted Child has done for you?

NAOMI [*in Adult*]: Well, I like what she's done for me—when it was necessary, yes.

DOCTOR: Do you have some nice things to say to her about that?

NAOMI *(long pause):* Not really . . . not really.

DOCTOR: She saved your life.

NAOMI: She saved my life, yes, but I feel sorry it was necessary—

DOCTOR: But wasn't it nice of her, though? I mean, when you needed her, to help you?

NAOMI: Yes, it was OK. Yes. You were there when I needed it. [*Speaking to Adapted Child.*] OK. When you gave me a poker face I was crying inside *(catch in voice).* But it isn't OK that I can still maintain a poker face and cry inside. I begin to resent that. I say, "What the hell, let me cry, let me do it: if I feel like wanting something, let me do it. And if I feel like reaching or needing or. . . . Don't give me that poker face—I don't want it. It isn't necessary anymore—"

DOCTOR: Be your Adapted Child again. What kind of recognition would you like to have?

NAOMI [*as Adapted Child*]: When you talk to me this way . . . when you talk to me this way I can't—

DOCTOR: How do you feel about yourself when you hear your Adult talk to you that way?

NAOMI: I kind of agree. I'm beginning to—uh—I sort of agree with you, Adult. I—I—ah—I have done my job, and now I guess I could go, I could disappear, or I could be replaced. I guess I'm not doing my job anymore.

DOCTOR [*speaking to Adapted Child*]: Would you like to change into something else?

NAOMI [*as Adapted Child*]: Of course I would like to change. I guess I would like to merge into your Free Child, Naomi. I would like to merge into your true Adult. And, if at all possible, which is much more difficult for you, Naomi, than anything else, merge into your Nurturing Parent.

DOCTOR: Would you be in your Nurturing Parent over on that other chair?

NAOMI: Talking to whom?

DOCTOR: Talking to your Adapted Child, and just express some appreciation.

NAOMI [*as Nurturing Parent*]: All right, Adapted Child, it's very hard for me, but I have a great deal of warmth for you. I guess it's hard for me to have a great deal of warmth for anyone, so you're not very different. I really do appreciate the fact that you made it possible for me to survive. And that you not only made me survive, but that you prevented me from falling apart completely ... that you kept the pieces together. I appreciate that, I really do.

DOCTOR: Be in your Adapted Child. How do you feel when your Nurturing Parent says that to you?

NAOMI: The appreciation? I think it's a little overdue.

DOCTOR: Do you accept the appreciation?

NAOMI [*still as Adapted Child*]: Yes, I seem to be able to have friendly feelings for you. I think I could even be friendly with you, if you express it in that manner.

DOCTOR: OK. Will you be in your Nurturing Parent? [NAOMI *moves to Nurturing Parent chair.*] Will you be friendly, will you accept that? Will you be friendly with your Adapted Child?

NAOMI [*as Nurturing Parent*]: Yes ... I'm kind of softening as I'm talking to you. Yes ... I could almost pat you on the head.

DOCTOR: Will you pat your Adapted Child on the head?

NAOMI: Yes. I will pat you on the head and say, "OK, little Adapted Child—you are OK with me, and, yes, I can be friends with you."

DOCTOR: What would you think if your Adapted Child gave some of her energy to your Free Child? Would you like that?

NAOMI [*in Free Child*]: Yes, yes, I would like that.

I would like a lot of free energy.

DOCTOR: Now be in your Adult and ask your Adapted Child if she would be willing to give some of her energy to your Free Child.

NAOMI [*in Adult*]: Will you give some of your energy to the Free Child? [*Answering in Adapted Child.*] I feel OK about it. [*Shifts to Free Child ego state.*] But I feel very strange about it.

DOCTOR: What's your fear?

NAOMI [*in Free Child*]: I'm almost afraid that without the Adapted Child I'm going to act ridiculous, I'm going to act crazy . . . that I'm going to act way beyond the stage I'm in. I'll be like a little animal let out of a cage, and I'm kind of fearful how I'll act. I don't know if I'll be able to handle it.

DOCTOR: OK. Well, your Adapted Child functioned very well in Belgium. It is very clever at knowing what's wrong, and how to behave. Right? How about your Adapted Child saving some energy to check up on your Free Child. So if your Free Child starts to go wrong, your Adapted Child can give her a nudge, and say, "Watch out." How would you feel about that?

NAOMI [*in Adapted Child*]: That sounds OK. I guess I could kind of police you a little bit.

DOCTOR: Would you give your Free Child some real freedom, though?

NAOMI [*in Adapted Child*]: Yes . . . if you don't get rid of me completely, and if you allow me to keep a little power, I'll give you more freedom and energy.

DOCTOR [*speaking to the Free Child*]: OK. Is that agreeable to you?

NAOMI [*as Free Child*]: Oh . . . it's *very* agreeable to me. I think that's terrific. I can't wait to be unleashed, and to let go. Because I've been pushed down for so many years. I don't know what I'll do, but . . . even now, I feel my feet moving and my body moving, and it's as if—ah— it's part of the freedom.

Naomi is beginning to get in touch with her Free Child and to accept the permission offered her in the group to enjoy herself. She still needs, however, to integrate the two parts of herself—Naomi the Jew and Mary Catherine the Catholic. She has been moving steadily in that direction, and a breakthrough is imminent.

What follows is a verbatim transcript of Naomi's work as taped on February 24, 1973—about six weeks later.

DOCTOR *(to* NAOMI): What do you want to work on today?

NAOMI: I would like to—uh—obtain a sense of self. I would like to find a self somewhere, an identity, and strengthen it. I fluctuate too easily . . . like what happened with Jane today. Uh—when we were doing the exercise of looking into each other's eyes, I made up my mind that I don't have to manipulate, that I don't have to give to be accepted or to want something. And I was able to do it finally with Jane—to be conscious that I don't have to give, that I don't have to be different, I can just be me. But afterwards she started to cry, and then she got me into crying, and I really—and I couldn't help myself, I said, "Jane, as nice as it was, I feel very vulnerable"—and—uh—I don't like to be vulnerable. I'm very unsteady when I am vulnerable. And I can't seem to fall back on myself, to say, OK, I can be vulnerable for two minutes and then fall back on the self. I don't seem to find a self to fall back on. That makes me feel uncomfortable. Also, when I'm vulnerable, I don't feel safe at all.

DOCTOR: How don't you feel safe?

NAOMI: Uh—because I feel that I would like to trust, and at that particular moment I can't. *(Pause.)* But then I guess I feel I'm going to get kicked, at the same time, you know.

DOCTOR: Do you trust the feeling that if you trust somebody you'll get kicked?

NAOMI: No, I don't trust that feeling either completely . . . no. I'm somehow nowhere.

DOCTOR: All right, go to five people—just pick five people out—and say, "If I trust you, I'm afraid you'll kick me." Will you do that? Have a little exchange about it.

NAOMI: I would like to put it in a little different way. I believe I trust you. I feel myself becoming vulnerable. And when I'm vulnerable I don't know what to expect. *(Going to* EVELYN.*)* I trust you, but I feel vulnerable.

EVELYN: You really mean that, Naomi?

NAOMI: I trust you, but still . . . I feel very vulnerable then, yes. *(Going to* SANDY.*)* I trust you, Sandy. I feel myself becoming extremely vulnerable. And when I'm very vulnerable I don't know what to expect.

SANDY: You don't need to be frightened of me.

NAOMI: Tom, I feel myself becoming vulnerable. I feel vulnerable. I don't know what to expect.

TOM: I understand how you feel.

NAOMI: Pat, I feel myself becoming vulnerable, and when I feel vulnerable I haven't got the faintest idea what I can expect, uh—from you. (PAT *hugs her.)*

DOCTOR: OK. I want to say something.

NAOMI: Yeah?

DOCTOR: If you trust somebody, really, you *are* vulnerable.

NAOMI: Yeah, I feel it.

DOCTOR: You'll never get out of that, either. Because if you really trust somebody, or you *really love* somebody, they can leave you, or they can turn against you, or they can do any number of things.

NAOMI: Uh-huh. *(Assenting and nodding her head.)*

DOCTOR: And you really are vulnerable, if you want to trust. If you don't want to trust, you can be isolated. Now I'll tell you what my experience is. Life's risky. Any way you look at it, it's risky. And I prefer to have experiences that matter to me. Therefore, I prefer to trust and I prefer to love, and I know I'm taking a risk, but I would rather take the risk, even if I lose the trust and love later, because I would rather experience it now. One problem that you have is that you get into the future, or you are reminded of the past, and you don't see the present; therefore, you can't experience in the present. You only experience your fears, not what's really there. Now, for me, I prefer to experience what's there. I prefer to experience someone I feel close to and trust. I don't know what's going to happen. I care, but not in a way that makes me afraid to risk. Now, how do you feel about that?

NAOMI: Yeah—uh—it's easy to understand, it makes a lot of sense, except I feel that—let's say—you gave an example about yourself—let's say that *you* take a chance and you are kicked in the behind by the person—I'm just saying that this might happen. *You* have a self, a strong identity of a self to fall back on. I don't feel I have that.

DOCTOR: What have I got that you haven't got?

NAOMI: My childhood was so different from yours. Nobody was out to get you.

DOCTOR: Well, I'm not so sure about that, or, to put it more correctly, I didn't used to feel so sure. My parents sent me from a rather poor community to a very wealthy one to go to grammar school and high school. I felt like an outsider, too. Of course, no one was really out to kill me, but I went into psychological hiding. I cut myself off from my peers.

NAOMI: From the time I was in the second grade I didn't *have* any peers. The first grade was integrated, but not after that. I was a Jew in a Catholic community, and after the first grade that's the way I was treated—rejected and isolated. I had peers in the first grade, but then I lost them.

DOCTOR: So it's very difficult for you to get a concept of yourself without peers, because you get the concept in relation to peers and what they play back to you.

NAOMI:    And it's also much more difficult because at home my family made me something which the outside world didn't.

DOCTOR:    Yes . . . what's that?

NAOMI:    My parents thought I was very special.

DOCTOR:    You can stick to that.

NAOMI:    Then when I put my foot outside, it wasn't so.

DOCTOR:    Will you say, "My parents were right, and the outside world was wrong about me."

NAOMI *(long pause):* Well, as their child, they thought I was special, I don't know.

DOCTOR:    Say, "As their child, I was special to them."

NAOMI:    Well, as their child, I was special to them, yes.

DOCTOR:    Will you say it?

NAOMI:    Yes. *(Pause.)*

DOCTOR:    They were right, and the outside was wrong. Will you say that?

NAOMI:    As their child, I was special to them, and they were right, and the outside was wrong. But it doesn't sound—it doesn't—

DOCTOR:    Sound good?

NAOMI:    No. It isn't reality, you know.

DOCTOR:    Well, say, "They were right, as their child, I was special to them, but the outside was right, too." Try it that way, and see if you like that better.

NAOMI:    That isn't what sounds better; it's what was reality.

DOCTOR:    Do you accept the mores of the society you lived in? Or don't you?

NAOMI:    If I accept them or not, I have no choice, do I? Or did I? At that time I had no choice. Yes, I did accept their values at the time. Yes, I very much accepted them, yes. I didn't think there was anything else.

DOCTOR:    All right, so—

NAOMI: Even my father said that the Jew was a dirty Jew. If my father said it, how can I—?

DOCTOR: So you feel like a dirty Jew, or did, anyway.

NAOMI: Yes, I did, very much so *(voice choking).* I think my father emphasized it more even than the outside world.

DOCTOR: OK. *(Voice low and somewhat discouraged, but picking up right away with the following remark.)* You want to be a dirty Jew?

NAOMI *(long pause):* I have eliminated the word dirty. Let's say it that way. But I still don't know if I am a Jew or Gentile. (NAOMI *is speaking very rapidly, as if under pressure.)* I don't know what I want to be, really, when it comes down to the nitty-gritty. It was the Catholic religion that I . . . that was drummed into me, and I accepted it, and it was an escape. My God, when I say, "My God," it was almost literally. It was everything that I needed at the time, I think. And wanted. It was almost a fantasy come true. It was something I fantasized on before the war— yeah—and it became a reality.

DOCTOR: So you had two selves, then—. You had the Catholic self and you had the Jewish self.

NAOMI: Right.

DOCTOR: OK.

NAOMI: Right. Except that the Jewish self was not anything at all, because my father wouldn't accept himself as a Jew.

DOCTOR: Wouldn't accept that either?

NAOMI: No. My parents, no, didn't accept themselves as Jews, no. Not at all.

DOCTOR *(grunts):* Uhm. *(Pause. Wonders where to go next, and goes through process of getting in touch with his feelings.)*

NAOMI: So I was always . . . I didn't know who I was.

DOCTOR *(rallying, with a sudden plan that came to*

*him):* Will you be your Catholic self, in that chair, and talk to your Jewish self, and say to each other what you think about each other?

NAOMI *(plays role of Catholic self):* Well, little Jewish girl, I don't really know very much about you. You're really a stranger to me. I'm not very comfortable with you *(sniffing).* And yet you're dear. That's the strangest thing. I can't even remove you. If I could put you aside, I think I might just do that. I tried to at one time.

DOCTOR: What happened when you tried . . . when you did try to put the little Jewish girl aside?

NAOMI: Happened? *(Weakly.)* I became extremely alienated from myself. I—I—during the war, I had to, of course, and it was very valid then, but after the war in college—I was in a Catholic college—I didn't have to keep the name Mary Catherine Jessen, and yet I did. A name that isn't mine, a name that was given to me during the war, and I just kept it.

DOCTOR: Whose name is Naomi?

NAOMI: Naomi is my name.

DOCTOR: Did you hear what you said?

NAOMI: I said Naomi is my name.

DOCTOR: It's your real name, right? So you have a real identity, then.

NAOMI: Yeah, it's the name I'm born with.

DOCTOR: OK. *(Reflectively.)* Well, talk some more.

NAOMI *(pause):* I'm growing into Mary Catherine right now. I'm beginning to hate that Naomi.

DOCTOR: You're beginning to hate?

NAOMI: Uh-huh.

DOCTOR: Be Naomi now. How do you feel about being hated, Naomi?

NAOMI: Well, I don't understand it *(voice choking).* I mean, I—ah—I wish I could put up an argument, I wish . . . I have no defense against it. I—uh—I don't understand it. I don't understand why *you . . . hate . . . me. (Words said slowly, and with feeling.)*

DOCTOR: Be Naomi and tell Mary Catherine, "I'm

all right. I'm an all right person. I have feelings."

NAOMI: I'm all right; I mean, I even choose to be ... but I am.

DOCTOR: "I hurt, I care."

NAOMI *(explaining):* I hurt, I care. *(Pause.)*

DOCTOR: Be Mary Catherine now. How do you feel about Naomi hurting and caring and being a person, Mary Catherine?

NAOMI *(being Mary Catherine):* I don't particularly care. I understand, but I don't seem to care. I would like to tell her, "You don't exist. Just go away. I don't want to have any part of you." *(Scornfully, with a looking-down-the-nose voice.)*

DOCTOR: OK. Now be Naomi and keep saying, "I do exist, I am real, I do exist, I am real."

NAOMI: I do exist and I ... and I ... am real. I do exist and I ... am ... real *(saying each word slowly).* I do exist, I am real. I am vulnerable. *(Long pause.)*

DOCTOR: "I do hurt."

NAOMI: I do hurt.

DOCTOR: "I can love ... but I'm afraid to."

NAOMI: I would like to love. *(Pause.)* It costs too much ... but I would like to love. Yes.

DOCTOR: Be Mary Catherine now.

NAOMI: All right.

DOCTOR: Can't you feel any sympathy for that poor little Jewish girl?

NAOMI *(playing role of Mary Catherine; voice choked):* Yes. But you see, you'll never be loved. *(Long pause.)*

DOCTOR: Tell her why.

NAOMI *(still playing Mary Catherine role):* Because you are not going to be accepted as you are for what you are. And you know it. Why do it over and over and over again? You have become a burden to me.

DOCTOR: Be—uh—be—uh *Naomi. (Said with emphasis.)*

NAOMI *(no response; long pause.)*

DOCTOR *(speaking for* NAOMI*)*: "You're wrong, Mary Catherine, and I'm going to prove it to you now. I'm in America, and Jews are accepted. My husband loves me, my children love me, I'm in a group. The people in the group love me, the people care about me and tell me that they like me. So you are *wrong*. I just want you to know you are wrong about that." Will you say that, Naomi?

NAOMI *(weakly)*: Well, Mary Catherine, you're wrong. I am no longer a little child. Very much of an adult, a woman who is very much loved by her husband, whose children turn to her and like her. *(Long pause.)*

DOCTOR: "I'm really quite a person."

NAOMI: As a matter of fact, maybe *you* are just the hindrance, right now. The one that's interfering.

DOCTOR: Be Mary Catherine now. *(Long pause.)* What do you feel about being a hindrance now, Mary Catherine?

NAOMI: Well, I don't like it. You must remember that I was the Gentile and you were the Jew, and I made you survive.

DOCTOR: OK. Be Naomi. (DOCTOR *searching for the appropriate direction.)* Are you willing to accept Mary Catherine? She mattered to you then.

NAOMI *(big sigh)*: Well, I would just like to integrate the two of them. You and me, as two related entities.

DOCTOR: OK. Would you ask Mary Catherine if she would like to—to join you?

NAOMI *(pause)*.

DOCTOR: And be friends with you?

NAOMI *(pause, weakly and softly)*: All right, let's put aside the Jew-Gentile bit. I have accepted you, Gentile bit.

DOCTOR: Well, be Mary Catherine now.

NAOMI *(pause)*.

DOCTOR: Are you willing to see reality, now? That you are very important for what you did for Naomi, and that Naomi is very important *for what she is now?* And that you can care about her and she can care about you? Are you willing to accept that?

NAOMI *(as Mary Catherine):* Yes, I'm willing to accept that. *(Her voice is somewhat puzzled and without feeling.)* Somehow I feel I want to dominate Naomi.

DOCTOR: Well—uh.

NAOMI: And Naomi's not sure whether she wants to be dominated.

DOCTOR: Be Naomi now.

NAOMI *(silence).*

DOCTOR: May I feed you a line? Say to Mary Catherine, "I don't need to dominate you. You don't have to dominate me either. I can be where I am, and we can be friends. We can be equals. You matter."

NAOMI: We must be friends. Of course we are equal. Yes, I needed you, Mary Catherine, I needed you very, very much. I needed you from the time I stepped outside our own house until the time I came to the United States. You had to be there to protect me—and you were of value.

DOCTOR: Mary Catherine, will you accept that as OK?

NAOMI *(as Mary Catherine):* Yes. I know I was of value. I can certainly accept that.

DOCTOR: You saved Naomi's life in Belgium, and Naomi can save your life in America. Can you be friends?

NAOMI *(suddenly switches roles; long pause):* Well, right now, at this particular moment, I have a very strong feeling of letting go of Mary Catherine.

DOCTOR: Letting go of Mary Catherine? (DOC-TOR *is surprised at this sudden turn of events, but keeps his voice even.)*

NAOMI: Just right now, I all of a sudden had a feeling Mary Catherine is an unnecessary load which I don't need anymore, not really.

DOCTOR: Say that to Mary Catherine.

NAOMI *(pause).*

DOCTOR: "You're an unnecessary load, I don't need it now."

NAOMI: Ah *(more energetically).* I don't need you

anymore. I don't want to need you anymore. Let's say it this way, I really don't *want* you anymore. I've loved you long enough. I've certainly given you your dues, over and over and over again, even when it wasn't necessary, and I—I *(pause)* you're infringing now. I don't want you anymore. I don't need you anymore.

DOCTOR:   All right, are you ready to say good-bye to Mary Catherine?

NAOMI:   Yes, I think I am.

DOCTOR:   All right, then, say all the nice things that you want to say before you tell her good-bye, and then say good-bye to her.

NAOMI *(pause):*   Well, you kind of stepped in when I was a little girl. Everybody prayed in school, and you weren't allowed to pray, so you went home, and you kind of went on your knees and prayed for me and made me feel important, made me feel at least that I belonged somewhere, to something, somehow ... you ... certainly ... helped me. You strengthened little Naomi, you gave me a religion that I needed very desperately at the time ... so that I had something to hold on to.

DOCTOR *(feeding* NAOMI *a line):*   "I appreciate that."

NAOMI:   Yes. I appreciate that part of me, that strength, yes.

DOCTOR:   But now—

NAOMI:   It's not necessary anymore. I—ah—

DOCTOR:   So I want to say good-bye to you.

NAOMI *(pause):*   I want to say good-bye to a very old and dear friend. I am going to say good-bye to you. I—ah—the two of us can't make it. It's just got to be one of us. *(Voice choked and full of emotion.)*

DOCTOR:   Will you be Mary Catherine?

NAOMI *(long pause).*

DOCTOR:   Is it OK to say good-bye to Naomi, Mary Catherine?

NAOMI *(playing Mary Catherine's role):*   Yes. I'm ready to go. Yes, I'm ready to go.

DOCTOR: Where are you going to go?

NAOMI: Well, my strength is Mary Catherine. My good sense is Naomi.

DOCTOR: Will you merge your strength into Naomi, then?

NAOMI *(still playing Mary Catherine's role):* That part will merge, which is a good thing. Naomi, you are very, very lucky that you can put away a real hell that you have created in your mind, that a hell of a society created for you—ah—it's easy to put that part aside. It feels easy, anyway, to put that part aside.

DOCTOR: Be Naomi. (NAOMI *switches chairs.*) Say, "I'm going to accept the part of you that's good for me, and say good-bye to the fake part. I don't need that. I can be where I am now."

NAOMI: I'm accepting the part, the good part, which is me. The good part was the survival part, the mental survival part, the emotional survival part, and the physical survival part. I'm glad I could play the game. I'm going to keep that strong part, and . . . I'm going to let go of the fake part. I don't need that. As a matter of fact, I—I don't want it.

DOCTOR: OK. Will you say good-bye to it now, then?

NAOMI: Yes. Good-bye, Mary Catherine Jessen. You were OK when I needed you.

DOCTOR: "You served me very well, and I love you, and now I can say good-bye to you."

NAOMI: You served me very, very well, indeed— before we were done, you served me well. I'm grateful for the survival part, especially.

DOCTOR: Now can you feel the strong part of Mary Catherine merging into you? Can you feel it?

NAOMI: I don't know if it's a merging. I just feel very strong, something *strong* in *me*.

DOCTOR: That's you.

NAOMI: That's me, of course. That's me.

DOCTOR: How are you feeling?

NAOMI    *(pause):* I feel—

DOCTOR:    You feel?

NAOMI:    I *feel.* I don't know what I'm feeling, but I feel.

DOCTOR:    Go around and experience your feelings with everybody in the group. *(There were seventeen group members.)* Just experience everybody. Just feel.

[Most of this exercise was carried out silently. The group members stood up and held out their arms when Naomi came to them, and hugged her quietly in this moment of deep appreciation and warmth. Their comments were low and intimate: "It's beautiful." "It was really powerful work. You were beautiful." "I want to tell you how much I appreciate you." "I wanted you to do this." "I have a great deal of feeling for you. . . . I appreciate what you did." After making the rounds, Naomi came to me.]

DOCTOR:    Welcome, Naomi. *(Holds her close to him for about a minute.)* Now I would like you all to imagine you have a glass of wine in your hand, and we'll drink a toast to Naomi.

*(The group members, smiling, hold up their imaginary glasses.)*

DOCTOR:    I want to offer a toast to Naomi. Naomi, I'm very happy to have you with us again.

Naomi had now gone through all the deeper phases essential to her recovery. Although the pathology she presented initially was unusually severe, each patient, in his own way, goes through similar stages in therapy.

Transactional Analysis, Gestalt Therapy and nonverbal techniques, together with the psychoanalytic methods of free and directed association, when used conjointly, are powerful facilitators of change. Moreover, there is no conflict between any of these methods when they are used fluidly according to the therapeutic need.

In the end, however, it is the patient who is responsible

for change. The techniques help, even make possible the change, but it is the patient who changes. Unless the patient wants to change and seriously works toward it, he will not change.

From the beginning of treatment, Naomi showed that she wanted to change. She assumed a responsible position toward it. She always reported accurately what she thought and felt, and never pretended to be different at any moment than she really was. She always kept searching for and pushing for the integrations that she finally achieved.

# CHAPTER
# 8

## How You Can Begin to Change Yourself

You are probably aware, as I am, of the profound change that Naomi experienced in the process of her integration and discovery of her own identity. This did not happen by accident. It happened as the result of specific techniques used flexibly to meet the needs she had during each phase of her therapy, in conjunction with her own powerful motivation to change.

It may not have been so easy to recognize the specific techniques used, however, since they were not identified when used, and one ran flexibly into another during the group process.

I will now describe some of these various techniques separately, isolate them, tease them out, as it were, and present them in the form of exercises, or questions, which may be helpful to you. I have used them myself, found them beneficial in facilitating change in me, and perhaps this will also be the case with you.

### SENSORY AWARENESS

The following are exercises designed to help you get into the "here and now," a state of mind in which all of your attention is centered upon whatever is happening at the moment.

1. *Body-awareness exercise.* This exercise is described in detail in Chapter 2. Repeat it every day for one week. When you finish, each day, sit quietly and experience how you feel. When I do this, I experience a sense of relaxation and peace.

2. *Eye-to-eye contact.* Find a partner—perhaps your spouse, a friend, lover, or someone else. Who it is doesn't matter, so long as that person cooperates with you. Sit opposite her or him at a comfortable distance, perhaps three feet. Now, each of you look into the other's eyes for about three minues. Do not talk. Just look into your partner's eyes steadily.

When you do this, you will probably go through a whole variety of experiences, as I do. First you may be anxious about what your partner is experiencing. You may feel embarrassed and want to look away. Don't look away, just keep looking into your partner's eyes. As I continue to do this my anxiety goes away and I almost feel drawn into my partner's eyes, and I experience a sense of peace and quiet. When I reach this state, I am in the "here and now." I am observing and experiencing, existing in the act of merely recording and acknowledging what I see.

3. *Palm-to-palm contact.* "Getting to know the other person's hand without talking and with your eyes closed." For full instructions, refer to Chapter 2. During this exercise, keep all extrinsic thoughts out of your head. Experience only the sensations of exploring your partner's hand. Only then will it be a "here and now" exercise. Repeat if you desire, either with the same or another partner.

4. *The "blind walk."* Refer to Chapter 2. The point of this exercise is to experience whatever you touch in a non-stereotyped, fresh way. Afterwards, share your experiences with your partner.

These are all sensory awareness exercises, designed to increase your awareness of yourself and of others. Did you feel comfortable doing them? Did any of them embarrass you? If so, it was probably because of some parental message such as "Don't have feelings," "Don't trust" or "Don't be close." They are valuable in helping you discover how you keep yourself from being in the "here and now."

## STROKING

As you know, strokes are units of recognition. Here are three exercises that will help you become aware of the effect of positive unconditional and positive conditional strokes on yourself and on others. (Refer to Chapter 4 to refresh your memory about TA concepts.)

1. *Give five positive strokes a day to other people, for one week.* Notice their response, and how you feel. Your stroke might be an honest compliment, a note of appreciation, a phone call to an old friend, a smile, a hug. There are many ways to convey your recognition, acceptance, and appreciation of others.

2. *Be aware of whether you are accepting or rejecting positive strokes.* It is difficult for people who learned as children to feel Not OK about themselves to accept positive stroking. Out of their awareness, they discount themselves and others. When someone gives you a compliment, do you inwardly shrug it off, saying to yourself, "Oh, she doesn't mean that," or, "He doesn't know what I'm really like"? It is important not to discount other people's honest feelings about you; let the good strokes "sink in," and own them.

3. *Give yourself three positive strokes every day for a week.* I have found in my practice that this is a difficult

exercise for many people to do. They "forget" or they "don't have time" or they "feel silly." They can hear parental tapes playing in their heads, saying, "Don't brag," "Don't be vain," and so forth. This is a sure way to rob yourself of the joy of accomplishment. Whenever you do a job well, for example, you deserve to say to yourself, "I did that well." Enjoy your success!

A good way to practice giving yourself positive strokes is to place two chairs facing each other. Be in your OK Nurturing Parent in one chair, and put your Child (the child you used to be) in the other chair. Then give your Child three positive strokes. For example, "I like you; you're very bright; you're a winner." Then switch chairs, be in your Child ego state, and find out if the Child heard and accepted the positive strokes. This exercise draws energy to both your OK Nurturing Parent and your Free Child, and in this way you can begin to modify the Not-OK feelings in the Child aspect of your personality.

As you continue your practice you may find that there is so much pleasure in giving and receiving positive strokes that you won't need to remind yourself to practice. You'll be doing it naturally.

## EGO STATES: PARENT, ADULT, CHILD

In order to understand yourself, it is important to learn to recognize your ego states.

*Parent.* One of the simplest methods of becoming familiar with our own Parent ego state in all of its aspects is to recall how our parents treated us both verbally and nonverbally.

Find some quiet spot, where you will not be distracted, and remember everything that you can about your parents' attitudes and behavior. As you do this it may help you to write down what you recall. Also write down what your reactions were. Do this every day for a week. Think about your parents' attitudes concerning the things that were important to you as a kid; for example, how they wanted you to treat them, how they taught you to treat your siblings, how they behaved at mealtimes and how you responded to them, what their attitudes were about discipline, money, clothes, school, helping with the household chores, work, play, sex, religion. At first allow all memories of these things to come up freely. Then organize them under the headings OK Nurturing Parent, Not-OK Nurturing Parent, OK Critical Parent and Not-OK Critical Parent.

Now think about the ways your own thinking, feeling, and behavior are affected by the "tapes" from your parents. Next, identify your own Parent ego states during your daily acitivties. Are you Nurturing, Overprotective, OK Critical or Not-OK Critical?

*Adult.* As Berne states, the function of the Adult is to appraise the environment and work out the possibilities, probabilities, and options. He even goes so far as to say that the Adult is the ego state that makes survival possible. It does this by collecting information, processing the data collected, and using this as the basis for estimating the probabilities of any given course of action.

Make an effort to determine whether or not your Adult is contaminated by Prejudicial Parental messages, such as "You can't trust anyone these days," or Child delusions, such as "Some day my Prince (or Princess) will come, and then I will live happily ever after."

*Child.* Have a conversation with a partner about taking a vacation. Taking turns, play the role of the OK Free Child, the Not-OK Free Child, the OK Compliant Child, the Not-OK Compliant Child, the OK Rebellious Child and the Not-OK Rebellious Child. This exercise is fun.

## QUESTIONS TO INCREASE SELF-AWARENESS

### *Transactions: Complementary, Crossed, and Ulterior*

After carefully reviewing the section on transactions in Chapter 4, practice the three types with a partner.

### *Options*

Have a dialogue with your partner in which he angrily accuses you of always being late for a party. Is your first impulse to respond like an Adapted Child (Compliant or Rebellious) to a Critical Parent? Avoid getting hooked by responding from a different ego state than the one he addressed, or by directing your response to a different ego state in him. You may be surprised at the result.

### *The Dusay Egogram*

Draw your own egogram. If you would like to, invite several other persons whom you know well to draw your egogram. Then compare. Is there any difference between the way you think you relate to others and the way you really come across to them? Do you want to modify your egogram in any way?

### *Injunctions*

If you had difficulty performing any of the preceding exercises, it is probable that this goes back to your original injunctions. If you recognize any injunctions and have great difficulty getting rid of them, you may wish to seek a therapeutic group.

### *Early Decision*

Do you remember making an early decision about how to live your life? What was it?

### *Life Scripts*

Do you have a winner's, non-winner's, or loser's script? Do you have any one of the following losers' scripts: Never, Always, Until, After, Over and Over, and Open Ended? Reread the description of each one of these scripts in Chapter 4 and see whether the way you are behaving in your life fits into any one of them. Would you like to change your script?

### *Fairy Tales*

Think of a favorite fairy tale from childhood, or a favorite character in a book, television or motion picture show. Does your life script fit in with the way that character lived his life?

### *Miniscripts*

Did you receive any or all of the five counterscript drivers? Would you like to get out from under their influence? If you would, give yourself some allowers, as suggested by Kahler and Capers in their article on the "Miniscript." The allower for "Be perfect" is "It's OK to be yourself." The allower for "Hurry up" is "It's OK to take your time." The allower for "Try hard" is "It's OK to do it." The allower for "Please me" is "It's OK to consider yourself and respect yourself." The allower for "Be strong" is "It's OK to be open."

### Symbiosis, Discounting, and Passivity

Are you in a symbiotic relationship with anyone? Do you realize that symbiosis is maintained by discounting and passivity? Be aware that when others discount you, or "put you down," every discount needs to be confronted (realistic circumstances permitting) in your Adult ego state, in order to neutralize its effect and help you stay in your own power.

### Time Structuring

How much time do you give to withdrawal, rituals, activities, pastimes, games, and intimacy? Would you like to change the amount of time you spend in any one, or all, of these categories? How will you implement this?

### Rackets

Do you have any of the following rackets: depression, sadness, inadequacy, anxiety, confusion, anger, helplessness, fear, and guilt? Reread the section on rackets and identify yours. Be aware of them at the time they are actually seriously influencing your behavior. Do they serve any constructive purpose?

### Existential Positions

What is your existential position? If you are not satisfied with it, what steps can you take to move toward the "I'm OK–You're OK" position?

### Trading Stamps

Do you collect trading stamps (grudges)? If you do, what are the advantages to you? Disadvantages?

### *The Redecision*

Would you like to make a redecision? What are your real goals, and how do you want to accomplish them?

### *Contracts*

Will you make a contract to implement your redecision?

It is my hope that you will experience the exercises I have suggested, and seriously consider the questions I have raised. They will increase your awareness of yourself and others, and perhaps open up new options for change.

# CHAPTER
# 9

## *Essentials for Change*

Certain basic ingredients are essential for growth, in human beings as in all forms of life. Every infant is born with the innate capacity to develop and to actualize himself/herself. In the plant kingdom, every seed contains within itself the mechanisms that lead to its unfolding and becoming what it can become. Whether it becomes a pine tree or a rose, and what variety of pine tree or rose, depends upon its heredity—the chromosomes and genes, and within the genes the DNA and RNA which, following a genetic code, produce specific kinds of proteins.

But whether the pine tree becomes a specimen tree, a tall, straight, beautiful tree, with strong limbs that withstand powerful winds, and thousands of healthy pine needles that sigh in the summer breezes; and whether the rose becomes an unfolding thing of beauty, "a joy forever," depends upon other ingredients. It depends upon the nature of the soil, its acidity or alkalinity, the minerals it contains, upon the amount of light, and water it receives, and the quality of the air it breathes.

It is the same with the human infant. The capacity to grow and develop is inborn, but what kind of child and adult he grows into, and whether he will actualize himself and become what he can become, depends upon more than the essential ingredients for healthy physical growth, such as food, water, light, and air. The infant needs the psychological equivalent of these things as well.

How he will develop depends, upon other things, upon the emotional climate in which he is raised; that is, how he is treated by his parents or parental substitutes—whether he is given positive unconditional and conditional stroking, for example, or whether he receives negative unconditional stroking. Whether he is loved or hated, respected for himself or disregarded. As he grows up he needs to be stroked positively, he needs to be respected as a person who is worthwhile for himself.

If he does not receive these and other psychological necessities for healthy growth, he will not become psychologically whole until he *does* receive them in the present. What was missed in the past must be made up *now,* or he will remain fixated in his infantile or childlike psychological positions.

This means that the person needs to receive in therapy or in some other way those things, those basic psychological essentials, which he did not receive in the past. He needs to be loved, to be respected for what he is, to be listened to because what he says is important, to be told that he is worthwhile, to be given permission to change, and to be informed that the therapist will support him in this change.

This alone, however, is not enough to produce change, for very special reasons. Because the patient has been subjected to rejection and other forms of negative treatment in the past, he suffers a loss of trust and is unable to believe that he is being accepted and respected in the present, even when he is. No matter what the therapist does, the patient is apt initially to look upon it with suspicion.

This temporary impasse requires special techniques. The patient needs to learn (and therapy is a process of learning) that he does not accept the present as real because he was conditioned in the past to believe that only those attitudes and outlooks learned in the past are real—that is, effective for coping with current problems of living. Believing this, he is reluctant to let go of past habits of coping, even though he may feel dissatisfied, confused, or even frightened. He is unable, by himself, to see which part of what he learned in the past is now unrealistic and no longer to be trusted, and which part he can really depend upon as valid. The therapist helps him in the present to distinguish between what is real and what is unreal in his current life. For this, the methods of TA are unexcelled. They lead to an intellectual understanding, which is necessary if the patient is to release himself from the past.

But such intellectual understanding is not enough by itself to produce optimum change. This is because much of what has been learned was learned at a deeper level than the intellectual; it was learned initially at an emotional level, deeper than words. These deeper-level feelings need to be released, and they can be released using the methods of Gestalt Therapy and the techniques of nonverbal communication. Until this is done, the patient does not, in my experience, become free and autonomous.

In spite of his growing awareness of his need to change adapted patterns of behavior, the patient is frequently blocked by his fear of giving them up and risking new and more fulfilling ways of being.

The optimum place for such change to occur, in my experience, is in a controlled environment for personal growth, such as an ongoing TA/Gestalt/nonverbal communication group. This group becomes a new family and a therapeutic community. Such a community is not one in which everyone gives strokes to everyone else indiscriminately. Rather, the members feel free to give and to accept the kind of strokes they want.

In such an environment, group members feel free to exist, to be themselves, to belong, to be children, to grow up, to trust, to make it, to think, to be important, to have feelings, to show feelings, to be close, to be sane, and to enjoy themselves.

Having experienced these feelings, they learn to

incorporate them in their personalities and hence in their dealings with daily realities. They grow to feel like winners, and are in a much better position to become winners in life.

You will notice that each of the permissions I have just listed is the reverse of an injunction. The group is the best place that I know of to reverse the effect of the injunction, and also the best place to change, to have new experiences, and to grow.

And so the scene unfolds.

# CHAPTER
# 10

## *The Capacity to Change Is Intrinsic*

When I think over the events that led to the writing of this book, I am particularly impressed with two things: first, the immense capacity which human beings have for change, and second, the immense resistance which many human beings have to making it. Not that they purposefully and intentionally refuse to modify their personalities in ways that would be beneficial to them. On the contrary, they are the first to say, "I'm unhappy the way I am. I want to change." Then they add, "But I don't know how." Then, later in therapy when they do know how, they say, "I can't change; I try, but nothing happens." I help them along by saying, *"Can't* is a 'Child' word, and so is *try.* The Adult statement is *will* or *won't. Try* means, 'I'll try and if I don't succeed, please forgive me.' Nobody ever accomplished anything important by trying. Real change, such as you are working for, requires more commitment."

Then follows a long period of frustration.

It is as if the person is in the grip of an outside force, which impels him to remain unchanged, to continue to follow the early patterns of behavior. This is the conditioning effect of the injunctions.

Every time he attempts to do something constructive— such as show his feelings, or be close—he shies away from it, or does something to spoil it. For example, a woman who received the injunction, "Don't show your feelings," and who finally decides to show her feelings, makes an attempt to do so and what comes out is a burst of anger for which she gets kicked; and the man who received a "Don't be close to women" injunction, and who has come to the point where he wants to be close, is so frightened and clumsy that he does something which drives the other person away. I remember very well the case of a patient of mine, John, who, in recounting what happened on one of his first dates after coming into therapy and starting to get over his fear of being close to women, said, gleefully, "I kissed her so hard that I could hear our teeth click." That's the last time she ever let him kiss her; in fact, it was the last time she ever went out with him. His concept of how to be close to a girl was to squeeze her so hard that he could feel her ribs bend. He had psychological closeness and physical force mixed up. Underneath this was repressed anger.

Nevertheless, the thing for such a man to do is to persist. Persist in his efforts to get close to women in a different way, persist in taking risks to do so, and persist in therapy. John persisted and he is now married.

Some persons who are advanced in the process of therapy say, "I am so mad at myself because I have been suffering for so long. If I had only known what I know now twenty years ago." Such a person is staying in an anger racket—the last stand of the racket, so to speak. I say, "Let the past go. Be happy now."

I would like to come back to the immense capacity that human beings have to change. My experience is that at least 95 percent of the patients who come to work with me change radically, and if they remain in therapy long enough for the changes to be ingrained, they stay that way.

I was excited recently in a conversation with a friend of mine, who is a celestial navigator, by a phrase he used. He said, "I am impressed with the *immense precision of infinity.*

I can make a sight on a star, and know my position anywhere on the earth within hundredths of an inch."

That blew my mind.

I have thought of this often, and in the process have come to recognize more fully what I have known for a long time—that the human mind is perhaps equally as precise. *I am impressed with the immense precision of the human mind.* Eric Berne has pointed this out again and again in his books. Given the early scene and the character of the early negative conditioning, one can predict, within limits, the nature of the life script and the way it will be lived, unless some happy intervention changes it.

A person does not need—inevitably—to remain in a loser's script. The capacity to change and to learn is intrinsic. Getting over the effect of the injunctions is a process of learning. At first a process of unlearning, and then a process of learning anew—learning a new way of life and learning to take risks to achieve and possess it.

Hence the efficacy of the controlled environment for personal growth, such as in ongoing TA, Gestalt, and nonverbal communication groups, in marathons, and in week-long and month-long workshops.

I believe in the process of growth and change because it happened to me *("I* happened to me") and is still happening, and I see the process taking place in my groups all the time.

We know now what to do in order to facilitate the growth of the capacity for autonomy and intimacy and the existential position "I'm OK—You're OK." You can choose to do these things if you want. I choose to do them in order to own my own life.

# *Notes*

INTRODUCTION

1. F. S. Perls, *Gestalt Therapy Verbatim* (Lafayette, California: Real People Press, 1969), p. 28.

CHAPTER 1

1. Perls, *Gestalt Therapy Verbatim,* p. 4.

CHAPTER 3

1. F. S. Perls, *Gestalt Therapy Now,* ed. Joen Fagan and Irman Lee Shepherd (Palo Alto, California: Science and Behavior Books, 1970), p. 16.
2. Perls, *Gestalt Therapy Verbatim,* pp. 55-56.
3. Perls, *Gestalt Therapy Now,* p. 22.
4. Perls, *Gestalt Therapy Verbatim,* p. 52.
5. Perls, *Gestalt Therapy Now,* p. 26.
6. Perls, *Gestalt Therapy Now,* p. 22.

CHAPTER 4

1. Eric Berne, *What Do You Say After You Say Hello* (New York: Grove Press, 1972), p. 85.
2. Berne, *What Do You Say,* p. 11.
3. Berne, *What Do You Say,* p. 12.
4. Berne, *What Do You Say,* p. 12.
5. See Stephen Karpman, "Options," *Transactional Analysis Journal* 1:1 (January 1971): 79.
6. John M. Dusay, "Egograms and the Constancy Hypothesis," *Transactional Analysis Journal* 2:3 (July 1972): 37-41.
7. Berne, *What Do You Say,* p. 21.
8. Harry Frederick Harlow, Ph.D. Director of the Wisconsin Regional Primate Research Center.

9. R. Spitz, "Hospitalism," in *Psychoanalytic Study of the Child,* 1 (1945): 53-74.

10. Berne, *What Do You Say,* pp. 21-22.

11. See Eric Berne, *Transactional Analysis in Psychotherapy* (New York: Grove Press, 1961): p. 99.

12. Berne, *What Do You Say,* p. 23.

13. Berne, *What Do You Say,* p. 23.

14. S. B. Karpman, "Script Drama Analysis," *T. A. B.* 7:6 (April 1968): 31-43.

15. Eric Berne, *Games People Play* (New York: Grove Press, 1964).

16. Berne, *What Do You Say,* p. 25.

17. Berne, *What Do You Say,* p. 446.

18. Claude Steiner, *Games Alcoholics Play* (New York: Grove Press, 1971), p. 48.

19. These injunctions are the ones I learned from Robert and Mary Goulding at the Western Institute for Group and Family Therapy during a workshop in August 1972. They are presented and discussed by Robert Goulding in an article entitled, "New Directions in Transactional Analysis: Creating an Environment for Redecision and Change," in *Progress in Group and Family Therapy,* edited by Clifford J. Sager and Helen Singer Kaplan, Brunner/Mazal, 1972.

20. See Goulding, "New Directions in Transactional Analysis," p. 111.

21. See Eric Berne, *Sex and Human Loving* (New York: Simon and Schuster, 1970), pp. 164-167.

22. F. Kahler and H. Capers, "The Miniscript," *Transactional Analysis Journal* IV:1 (January 1974): 26.

23. See Berne, *What Do You Say,* pp. 85-86.

24. See Berne, *What Do You Say,* p. 86.

25. See Aaron Wolfe Schiff and Jacqui Lee Schiff, "Passivity," *Transactional Analysis Journal* 1:1 (January 1971): 71.

26. Schiff, "Passivity," p. 75.

27. See Goulding, "New Directions in Transactional Analysis," p. 118.

CHAPTER 6

1. Perls, *Gestalt Therapy Now,* p. 22.

# Index